CROSSING THE RIO GRANDE

D1568478

NUMBER NINE: GULF COAST STUDIES
Sponsored by Texas A&M University–Corpus Christi
John W. Tunnell Jr., General Editor

CROSSING THE RIO GRANDE

An Immigrant's Life in the 1880s

LUIS G. GÓMEZ

TRANSLATED AND WITH COMMENTARY BY
GUADALUPE VALDEZ JR.
INTRODUCTION BY THOMAS H. KRENECK
EDITED BY GUADALUPE VALDEZ JR.
AND THOMAS H. KRENECK

Texas A&M University Press
College Station

The paper used in this book meets the minimum requirements
of the American National Standard for Permanence
of Paper for Printed Library Materials, Z39.48-1984.
Binding materials have been chosen for durability.
♾

Library of Congress Cataloging-in-Publication Data

Gómez, Luis G.
    [Mis memorias. English]
    Crossing the Rio Grande : an immigrant's life in the 1880s / Luis G.
Gómez ; translated and with commentary by Guadalupe Valdez Jr. ;
introduction by Thomas H. Kreneck ; edited by Guadalupe Valdez Jr.
and Thomas H. Kreneck.—1st ed.
        p. cm. — (Gulf Coast studies ; no. 9)
    "Mis Memorias originally published in 1935 by Gorena Press, Rio
Grande City, Texas"—T.p. verso. Includes index.

    1. Gómez, Luis G. 2. Mexican Americans—Texas, South—Biography.
3. Immigrants—Texas, South—Biography. 4. Texas, South—
Biography. I. Valdez, Guadalupe Jr. II. Kreneck, Thomas H. III. Title.
IV. Series.
    F395.M5G66 2006
    976.4'0616872073—dc22

                                            2005037457

    ISBN 978-1-60344-808-6 (paper)

Mis Memorias originally published in 1935 by Gorena Press
Rio Grande City, Texas

Contents

Illustrations

Preface

*M*IS *MEMORIAS* CAME to my attention at a 1991 meeting of the Spanish American Genealogical Association (SAGA) in Corpus Christi when Guadalupe Valdez Jr. gave a formal presentation on the book. Luis Gómez was Valdez's grandfather, and as Valdez's commentary details, the two had a special relationship. At that SAGA meeting, Valdez showed the audience one of approximately five known extant copies. He was keenly interested in sharing these memoirs with researchers and was justifiably proud of his grandfather's literary and historical contribution. After I expressed the interest of the Special Collections and Archives at Texas A&M University–Corpus Christi in obtaining one of these rare items (online catalogs did not reveal one in the holdings of any library), Valdez soon generously donated one of the family's remaining copies to our institution. Following subsequent conversations, Valdez agreed to translate *Mis Memorias* into English for publication and to include a translator's commentary. Though a difficult undertaking, for him this project was naturally a labor of love and family devotion. He has done what everyone should do: that is, carefully listen to one's elders, remember and preserve that which is meaningful, and pass that wisdom and experience down to future generations.

Thus, this current publication of *Mis Memorias* is truly a product of two men: Luis G. Gómez and Guadalupe Valdez Jr. Courteous and correct in his demeanor, educated and dedicated to learning, Valdez is a consummate gentleman, possessing characteristics doubtless in the tradition of his grandfather. To know Guadalupe Valdez Jr. and to read *Mis Memorias* would lead anyone to recognize similarities between the two men.

By making these memoirs available to a wider audience, Valdez has done much not only for his grandfather's memory and for his family's heritage but for scholarship as well. He went about his translator's duties with ability, diligence, and perseverance. The English-reading and scholarly communities owe him a great debt. While it is a rare occurrence to locate such a piece of printed Mexican American literature that is heretofore unknown to libraries, it is also notable to have a direct descendant of the author who would devote such effort to translating and having it republished. The Special Collections and Archives of Texas A&M University–Corpus Christi is gratified to be associated with this endeavor. We are likewise sincerely grateful to Guadalupe Valdez for donating a copy of *Mis Memorias* and making this publication project possible.

Although Valdez will comment extensively on his translation, some preliminary mention of the editorial decisions might be made here. For one thing, we moved Gómez's original table of contents from the back to the front of the book for the reader's convenience. While aiming for clarity and readability, Valdez smoothed his grandfather's wording in places when a literal translation would not do justice to the author's meaning. Following the publisher's wishes, Valdez and I polished the translation to further facilitate the volume's accessibility. The present volume was also given a more descriptive title, *Crossing the Rio Grande: An Immigrant's Life in the 1880s*.

Valdez's work was strengthened substantially by Javier Villarreal, who provided editorial assistance with the initial translation. Professor of Spanish at Texas A&M University–Corpus Christi, Villarreal not only boasts the requisite academic expertise but also has a personal background that brings an important sensitivity to Luis Gómez's words and meaning. Raised in the Texas-Mexico border region, Villarreal possesses a cultural knowledge of and affinity for this binational, bicultural subject. He has sought to balance the spirit of Valdez's translation with what he saw in Gómez's original Spanish. Villarreal's comments on his editorial style are incorporated in his footnote 5 in chapter 7 of Gómez's text.

The wealth of expertise that went into translating Gómez's memoirs notwithstanding, we of course invite curious readers to compare this present English work with the Spanish-language original.

To further enhance the message of the book, we have included photographs and other visuals. Moreover, the introduction provides some background information on La Imprenta Gorena (Gorena Press) to amplify our understanding of the production of *Mis Memorias*. Thanks go to Alfonso C. Gorena of McAllen, Texas, and to George R. Gause Jr., head of Special Collections at the University of Texas–Pan American, for providing this essential material. Gorena also generously contributed a portrait of his father to accompany the background notes. In addition, we deeply appreciate the research assistance given by Casey E. Greene and Virginia Rigby of the Rosenberg Library in Galveston; Bill Stein, director of the Nesbitt Memorial Library in Columbus, Texas; and David J. Mycue of the Hidalgo County Historical Museum in Edinburg, Texas. As usual, Arnoldo De León of Angelo State University gave us invaluable editorial input and encouragement.

Let me add a note of gratitude to Special Collections and Archives staff members Grace G. Charles and Jan S. Weaver for their assistance. Charles clarified various parts of the translation in the early stages of this project. As always, both she and Weaver assumed extra duties and gave much encouragement to help bring this project to fruition.

Finally, this publication project owes special thanks to Sandra Harper, Texas A&M–Corpus Christi provost and vice president for academic affairs; Christine Shupala, library director; and Jorge D. Canales, Texas A&M university counsel. Harper provided crucial financial support during a significant phase in the editorial process, while Shupala was particularly helpful by administratively encouraging this effort. Canales brought to bear his considerable knowledge in making sure that all of the copyright issues were secure. These three people recognized the importance of this project as a cooperative effort of the university with the larger Corpus Christi and South Texas lay community.

In the following translator's commentary, Valdez more fully informs us about his grandfather, their relationship, and how, when, and why the original book came to be produced, including the reason behind Valdez's decision to translate this work. The reader will discover that *Mis Memorias,* issued here in English as *Crossing the Rio Grande,* is a worthy volume. Authored by an older man who remembered his first instructive years in Texas as an 1880s immigrant from Mexico and translated by his grandson (now an octogenarian), it is a solid addition to Texas and Mexican American literature and history.

Thomas H. Kreneck
Associate Director for Special
Collections and Archives
Texas A&M University–Corpus Christi

Introduction

Thomas H. Kreneck

THE INTERNATIONAL BORDER between Mexico and the
United States has always been a permeable one. Ever since
the boundary was established during the nineteenth century, people from Mexico have come north to live and work,
and Texas has been a principal destination. While most schol-
ars and other observers of Mexican migration to the Lone Star
State have understandably focused on post-1900 immigrants
because of their massive numbers and importance in the making of modern society, statistics indicate that the nineteenth
century also merits consideration. To illustrate this point, historians currently estimate that the population of Texas Mexicans rose from around 14,000 in 1850 to almost 164,000 by
1900, an increase that was largely due to immigration.[1]

Yet, little is known about these people who came to make
Texas their home before the turn of the twentieth century. Few
left sources in the form of letters and memoirs to permit historians to understand them better. Fortunately, the recollections
of Luis G. Gómez have come to light to help fill this gap.

As the following translator's commentary and text amply
relate, Luis G. Gómez arrived as an immigrant to Texas as a
young man in the mid-1880s, then spent the rest of his life
there. Educated and hardworking, he journeyed across Texas
from Brownsville to Corpus Christi, Houston, and many points
in between, making his way with resourcefulness and determination and filled with hope in a new land. In the last years of
his life, Gómez had the additional fortitude to commit his experiences to paper in Spanish and have them printed in 1935
as *Mis Memorias*, tomo 1 (volume 1), in Rio Grande City. The
publisher, a press called La Imprenta Gorena, was most likely

the printing shop owned and operated by Alfonso Gorena (1893–1953).[2] The events Gómez describes in these recollections occurred between 1884 and the early 1890s, before he had married and begun to raise a family. His memoirs cover a time period when the number of people of Mexican descent in Texas increased from around 71,000 (in 1880) to approximately 105,000 (in 1890).[3]

As such, *Mis Memorias* is a piece of hitherto unrecognized Texana and historical literature. It stands as a needed primary document chronicling the life of a Mexican immigrant during a significant but obscure era. In many ways, *Mis Memorias* is a transcribed and edited oral history. Though Luis Gómez wrote *Mis Memorias* as an elderly man, his words remarkably retain the voice of a young person—fresh, observant of life's small things, and filled with wonder at the daily events that constituted his existence. Also, the book reflects someone who held these youthful exploits dear. For him, as with many older folks that oral historians often encounter, the incidents of Gómez's youth were, in his own words, "printed in [his] soul with indelible characters" (from the prologue).

The volume speaks for itself, but certain elements in the text might be related here to help the reader anticipate and follow the narrative with greater ease. Gómez begins his personal story by recalling the moment he crossed the Rio Grande at Matamoros-Brownsville in 1884 almost as if the event signaled the beginning of life for him. He had come to seek his fortune. With business skills, he became a partner, the bookkeeper, and a contract procurer for the Tamez-Gómez Company, one of many such contracting operations that at that time supplied Mexican labor to help create the infrastructure that developed the Texas economy. The Tamez-Gómez Company fulfilled contracts to clear land, cut wood, build roads, lay railroad track, construct bridges, quarry rock, and the like. Along the way, Gómez encountered many people and had various experiences. After relating numerous personal adventures, he abruptly ends the volume (the first of a projected two-volume set) with the completion of a fence-building contract in the Yoakum, Texas, area.

Mis Memorias reveals much about Luis Gómez, the man. He was an educated person. His comments reveal, for example, that he had more than a passing knowledge of the history of Mexico and the place of Texas within that history. Yet, like so many other immigrants, he possessed a useable trade (i.e., he could barber). An optimist by nature, a quality no doubt necessary for an immigrant to successfully make his way in a strange land, Gómez demonstrates a philosophical bent; he pondered why people did good or ill to their fellow human beings. He reflected on what he called the "mysteries of human life that only our creator can penetrate!" (from chapter 1). Gómez was clearly someone who believed in Divine Providence and the essential nobility of people, though he knew they were capable of evil as well as good. He was an acute observer of human nature and the human condition even as he went about the ordinary business of his life. And he had a penchant for descriptive detail. Indeed, Gómez emerges as someone more concerned with his interpersonal relationships on a daily basis than with the so-called larger issues of his times or with the broader environment. Also, he refreshingly reveals no bitterness amid the trials and tribulations he endured.

Gómez wrote *Mis Memorias* with two purposes: principally to entertain but at the same time to be "of great help to the young" (from the prologue). In pursuit of both goals, the volume sheds light for subsequent generations on many far-reaching issues of the 1880s' Mexican immigrant experience in Texas. It illuminates what one might call the immigrant's rhythm of life, as Gómez lived a peripatetic existence in search of employment in various places and used whatever mode of transportation he could. It vividly demonstrates the immigrants' resourcefulness and enterprise and the ways these newcomers searched for fortune and opportunity. The author speaks to the variety of immigrant personalities he met, their stories, and their characters. The book relates how Mexican immigrants struck individual accommodation with the people they encountered, including large and small acts of kindness and generosity that made their lives bearable. Most important for Gómez, for example, was the relationship he developed with a couple he identifies by the name of Staford (or Stafford), whose courtesies to him made such an imprint that he recounts that interaction in painstaking detail. He chronicles the courtship and marriage of this husband and wife, thus preserving to the best of his ability an intimate history of these prominent Anglo Americans.

Of specific interest to many historians will be the manner in which *Mis Memorias* illuminates the lives of Mexican labor contractors. As principals in a labor-contracting venture, Gómez and his partner faced numerous vicissitudes. The author, for instance, notes things about the labor contractors such as their margin of profit, the number of people they employed, the way they procured jobs with Anglo employers and set their rate of payment, what wages they paid workers, how they recruited and communicated with their laborers, and the number of hours it took to complete the various contracts. When one considers that some of Gómez's contracts were for laying railroad track, his economic pursuits take on added meaning because the railroad industry played a seminal role for the Mexican American community as a whole. In terms of labor history, the book also shows how Mexican immigrants not only came north with talents and ability but also developed new skills as they made their way into the Texas workforce.

Through it all, *Mis Memorias* demonstrates the central importance of the immigrants' pursuit of economic gain. At the heart of all of their labor and wanderings was the desire, as Gómez notes, to "get out of being poor" (from chapter 5). Gómez even mentions how he sent money orders home to his parents in Mexico, a practice that has a contemporary ring. Underscoring the perils specific to Mexican immigrants, Gómez comments that the right even to collect one's salary was "always in doubt when the employees were Mexicans" (from chapter 1).

Gómez's narrative depicts Mexican immigrants of the 1880s as individuals rather than statistics. The author describes Mexican customs in the United States such as the formalities of courtship and marriage. He notes the simple pleasures that Mexican immigrants had as lonely men in boarding houses, conversing all night about lost riches in Mexico, faithful women waiting for them in their homeland, and the jobs they took to make a living. He is perceptive in helping us appreciate the many dimensions of immigrant life of the 1880s, including the

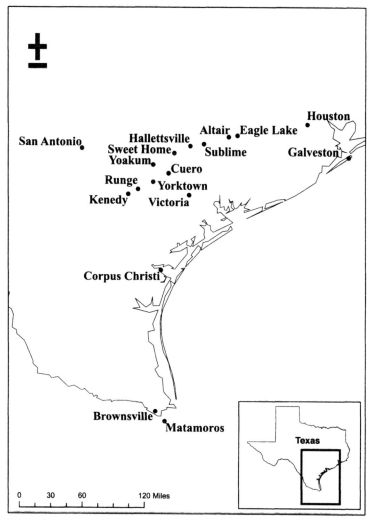

Map of area covered in *Mis Memorias* by Luis G. Gómez. Map by Richard Smith.

close relations of Mexicans with their Anglo employers, the way Mexicans were swindled at times by fellow Mexican workers, and the nights and days spent in solitude, peril, and desperation. He relates stories of supportive friendships among the immigrants, dealings between recent arrivals and *Tejanos,* and religious customs. He portrays simple home gatherings that may have served as the first social functions for those Mexican Texans who settled in urban regions (e.g., Houston) that were isolated from predominantly Mexican South Texas. For Gomez, the men and women with whom he chose to socialize—immigrants and native Mexican Americans alike—were people of substance and worthy of respect; he speaks of them as ladies and gentlemen no matter how modest their circumstances.

Gómez's personal memoirs further comment on the employment of single women in the Houston textile industry and the loss of the Spanish language by longtime Texas Mexican residents. His one major personal experience with an African American gives us a view of the unfortunate encounters between and attitudes of Mexicans and blacks. Through these insights and others, Gómez's modest reminiscences portray the Mexican immigrants of the 1880s as people with human strengths and foibles and thus a full measure of humanity. Indeed, the recollections of Luis Gómez add to our appreciation of the complexities of the Mexican immigrant experience.

A WORD ON THE ORIGINAL PUBLISHER

The publisher of *Mis Memorias* was probably Alfonso Gorena (1893–1953), who—when the book was published in 1935—owned and operated a printing shop in Rio Grande City. According to the recollections of his son, Alfonso Gorena was born in Mier, Tamaulipas. In 1915 he married Rosa Treviño in Camargo. Their first two children, both born in Mexico, died in 1918 during the great influenza epidemic. That same year, Alfonso Ciro Gorena, their third and oldest surviving child, was born in Camargo.[4]

The Gorena family had a tradition in the printing business in northern Mexico and the Rio Grande Valley of South Texas. Alfonso's father, Dionicio Gorena, had come to Mission, Texas, from Mexico to publish the local newspaper, *El Progreso,* around 1913 or 1914. Around 1919 (soon after the birth of their third child), Alfonso and Rosa Gorena also moved to Mission, where Alfonso, having learned the printing trade from his father, worked in a local print shop and one in nearby

Alfonso Gorena (1893–1953) of La Emprenta Gorena, ca. 1930s. Courtesy of Alfonso C. Gorena, Alfonso Gorena Photographs, Special Collections and Archives, Mary and Jeff Bell Library, Texas A&M University–Corpus Christi.

McAllen. Alfonso and Rosa would subsequently have six other children, all born in the United States.

Though the extent of his formal education is unknown, Alfonso Gorena was an intelligent person and an avid reader of works such as *The Count of Monte Cristo* and other great literature. After coming to Texas, he taught himself to speak, read, and write English. Prone to moving, he took his family from Mission to Monterrey, Nuevo León, where they lived for only five months before moving to Camargo, where they resided for a short time.

Gorena soon relocated his family to Rio Grande City, Texas, where he had been offered the job of editor and publisher of the *Rio Grande Herald* by the Manuel Guerra family, who owned the newspaper. When Gorena took the position, the paper was already in operation. He ran the *Herald* from about 1931 to 1935 and also served as the paper's linotype operator and manager of its small staff. Simultaneously, Gorena had his own small, separate printing shop in Rio Grande City. It was in this shop, under the name La Imprenta Gorena, that he probably produced Luis G. Gómez's *Mis Memorias* in 1935. During the 1930s, when Gorena became too ill to continue his work in Rio Grande City, he moved his family and printing equipment to Monterrey, where he reopened his small printing business. Gorena resided in Monterrey until 1953, when he died at age fifty-nine of a liver ailment.

Family tradition had it that Gorena left a small trunk filled with books and papers; however, family members lost track of it over the years. It is impossible to determine whether Gorena ever had possession of Gómez's second volume of *Mis Memorias* and, if so, what became of the manuscript. Nonetheless, La Imprenta Gorena played a role as publisher of volume 1 of Luis G. Gómez's *Mis Memorias* and thus made a substantial contribution to Spanish-language Texana.

NOTES

1. Arnoldo De León, *Mexican Americans in Texas: A Brief History*, 2d ed. (Wheeling, Ill.: Harlan Davidson, 1999), 36, 54.
2. See "A Word on the Original Publisher."
3. De León, *Mexican Americans in Texas*, 54.
4. The information is largely based on telephone interviews with Alfonso Ciro Gorena by Thomas H. Kreneck on November 20 and December 10, 2001. Born in 1918, Alfonso C. Gorena is the son of Alfonso Gorena and Rosa Treviño. At the time of these interviews, Gorena (who came to be called Alfonso Jr.) resided in Mission, Texas. On a March 1, 2002, visit with Gorena by Kreneck and Guadalupe Valdez Jr. to Gorena's home in Mission, Gorena also visually identified the original *Mis Memorias* volume as resembling work his father produced.

Memories of My Grandfather, Luis G. Gómez

Guadalupe Valdez Jr.

AFTER SO MANY years, it is impossible for me to remember how my first encounter with Luis G. Gómez, my grandfather, occurred. As I recall, it was around 1923, when I was six years of age, and I met him on the farm he worked near the little South Texas community of Ricardo, near Kingsville. Because I was his first grandchild and the eldest child of his only daughter, we quickly developed warm feelings toward one another. Perhaps it was a natural grandson-grandfather bond. To support our family, my own father was away working most of the time. As a result, my grandfather assumed a parental role in my life that only increased over time. Our association grew, and I developed a lasting respect, admiration, and love for him. He had a profoundly positive influence on my life. Without a doubt, the reverence that I feel for his memory accounts as much as anything else for my laboring so hard to translate his memoirs.

My grandfather was a remarkable man. My first remembrance of him is of a man in his mid-to-late fifties, standing about five feet eight inches in height, and weighing around 170 pounds. He had a ready smile and a rather dark complexion. He was a natural-born speaker and a community leader. He also enjoyed good conversation. It did not matter to him the age, gender, or ethnicity of the person with whom he conversed. When interested in a topic, he would be extremely engaging. If he were uncertain about the facts, he would use his natural ability to question and probe in order to satisfy his curious mind. Early in life, he also mastered both English and Spanish; this language proficiency as well as his ability to connect with people made his friends and acquaintances feel at ease in his presence. He was by nature an optimist.

According to his memoirs and what he told me, Luis Gonzaga Gómez was born on a hacienda near Linares, Nuevo León, in 1865.[1] His parents were likewise natives of that place. Of his ancestry I know only (again according to him) that he was one-eighth Yaqui Indian, something he claimed proudly. From Linares, his family moved to Matamoros, where he and his siblings were raised. My grandfather attended and graduated from a *colegio* in that border city.

Although my grandfather does not mention all of these circumstances in his memoirs, he told me that he left Mexico to escape political turmoil. In those days, skirmishes constantly took place between contending military forces, and much political conflict existed. When he graduated at eighteen years of age, he was vulnerable to being drafted into the army. To avoid getting caught up in the trouble, he and a friend and fellow student at the colegio decided to leave the country. Because their respective families also needed financial assistance, the two young men went to Texas seeking their fortune. Knowing my grandfather as I did, I think that he was also prompted to come north by an inner desire to spread his wings.

For his time, my grandfather was an educated man. His many talents suggest to me that during his youth he studied math, civil engineering, bookkeeping, and other practical subjects. I do not know whether the colegio that he attended was equivalent to our colleges today or more like a preparatory high school, but it provided him with an excellent education, as schools in Mexico customarily did in that era. By both training and nature, Grandfather was an intellectual who could converse on many topics. For instance, he was always ready to discuss the position of the stars on a clear summer night. The North Star was his favorite. Because he had traveled in unfamiliar country on many nights, that was his guiding beacon.

Grandfather's memoirs relate his many travels and adventures in Texas after he came here in 1884. He ended up in Shiner, Texas, where he met his future wife, Brígida Cano, who is mentioned at length in *Mis Memorias*.[2] After their marriage in 1892, they raised their family in Shiner. They had nine children: eight sons and one daughter. From oldest to youngest, these children included Apolonio (Paul), Carlos, Ben, Elisa (my mother), Trinidad (Trino), Manuel, Simón, Luis, and Gregorio (who died at birth). All eight of the surviving children attended school in Shiner and reached adulthood.

To the best of my understanding, my grandfather moved his family to Falfurrias around 1910. He went there at the invitation of Edward Lasater, founder of and the wealthiest man in Falfurrias. Lasater had heard about the good reputation of my grandfather and his partner, Eleodoro Tamez, as fence builders, road builders, and construction men. By this time, however, Tamez had decided to return to Mexico, so my grandfather came alone, with his family, to work with Lasater, but from what I heard as a youngster, Grandfather was apparently employed in Falfurrias for no more than a couple of years.

Around 1912 or 1913, my grandfather moved his family to Ricardo, which is about five miles south of Kingsville. He went there to rent and work a two-hundred-acre farm that belonged to the King Ranch. He rented this piece of ground as a *cuartero;* that is, he gave one fourth of what he raised to the King Ranch. On the farm, he raised cattle and planted cotton, corn, and redtop cane. The property had two houses, one where Grandfather and his family lived and one that was occupied by my mother and her husband, my father, who was named Guadalupe Valdez Sr.

My grandfather's wife, Brígida, my grandmother, died in Ricardo in 1917, the same year I was born. My grandfather never remarried and thereafter became both father and mother to his children.

At that time, few Hispanics attended college. Grandfather encouraged his children to become educated and inspired them by his actions. All eight of his children finished high school, and two of them graduated from college—Trino from St. Edward's University and Simón from what is now Texas A&M University–Kingsville. My mother was fluent in English and Spanish and zealously promoted education for her own children, a trait she doubtless inherited from her father. Of her six offspring, we all graduated from college. In fact, although I was the oldest, I was the last one of my mother's children to graduate, but she lived long enough to see it happen, which filled her with great satisfaction.

I was born in one of the houses on the King Ranch that my grandfather farmed, and we lived there for about a year. Our house was located maybe half a block from my grandfather's house. When my father received an offer to work on other King Ranch property on the north side of Kingsville, we moved and stayed there for five or six years. After that we moved back to Ricardo, again to live in the house next to my grandfather. That is when I first remember meeting and getting to know him. As I have mentioned, I was just a child, and my family's economic circumstances were difficult. With my father always away working hard, clearing land in the vicinity, and camped out for up to a week at a time, my grandfather became a primary influence on me.

Grandfather was a recognized figure in the Ricardo community. During the Christmas holidays, for example, our family would get together and make tamales and *chicharones* (pork cracklings). A generous person, he would invite friends and neighbors over to share these goodies with us. Because he was an effective public speaker, he gave talks at local schools during the Christmas holidays on the history of the Bible as it relates to Christmas. He knew the Bible thoroughly and could easily cite biblical passages in conversation. He was a Catholic and a believer, although he was not what one would call a regular churchgoer.

Anyone who needed assistance could count on my grandfather for help. Because he spoke both Spanish and English, members of the Ricardo Hispanic community would say whenever they had any problems, legal or otherwise, "Vamos a ver a Don Luis [Let's go see Don Luis]. He can help us out." And he always did his best to resolve the difficulties.

As a Catholic, Grandfather was also instrumental in building the first Catholic church in Kingsville—St. Martin's. To help construct the church, he raised funds. Whenever the parish needed money, he was there to assist.

Along the way my grandfather became a U.S. citizen, but he never forgot the nation of his birth. He always attended the Mexican national holiday celebrations around Kingsville, and at least once I heard him speak before a group assembled for such an occasion. He was very respectful of the Mexican government, although he did not always favor the actions of its leadership. He loved Mexico, but he also loved the United States. He was a true patriot.

My grandfather was instrumental in encouraging the community to support the founding of the South Texas State Teachers College in Kingsville, which first became Texas A&I and then, in 1993, Texas A&M University–Kingsville. He was very involved in helping to raise the funds needed to establish that institution. When the school was inaugurated in 1925, there was a panoramic group picture taken. I was there with my grandfather, but I have never been able to locate us in that photograph. Still, I remember that picture because he and I were there. My grandfather was very happy about the dedication. Numerous Mexican American people attended that ceremony, folks who had worked with my grandfather on the project. There was a friend of his named Flores, one named Solíz, and the Garcías. Everyone in the local Mexican American community was congratulating him, patting him on the back and telling him that he had done a good job. At the time, I was just a youngster and did not realize the importance of this event, but as I grew older, I realized its true significance.

The last time I saw my grandfather was in 1934. That year, he moved to Rio Grande City where one of his older sons, my Uncle Ben Gómez, resided. Unfortunately, I had to leave school in 1932, when I was in the ninth grade, to help my family during the Great Depression. I joined the Civilian Conservation Corps (CCC) in mid-1936 and immediately left the state. My grandfather and I simply never had a chance to see one another again.

In 1937 I was in Grants Pass, Oregon, with the CCC when a letter arrived from my mother. In it she told me that my grandfather Luis had passed away two weeks earlier. The news pained me so much that for a week I was prostrate from grief. I could neither eat nor sleep. I felt as though something had gone out of me. I kept doing my job, my project, but I was not always sure what I was doing. I was really hurting. My grandfather was laid to rest in Kingsville in the Chamberlain Cemetery alongside his wife, my grandmother.

When I had last seen him in 1934, however, he mentioned that he was writing two books. He related this in a conversation he had with me, his son Trino (who was just back from St. Edward's University), and his younger son Simón (who was attending college in Kingsville). But only the first of these volumes (tomo 1) of what he called *Mis Memorias* would be printed. By the time he told us about his writing project, my grandfather was already making plans to move to Rio Grande City to live with his son Ben. In 1935 he published the book in Rio Grande City, but I was soon gone to the CCC without knowing that it had appeared. It was not until around 1947 that I actually saw a copy of it. As readers will note in the first pages of the text, my grandfather briefly explains the nature and intent of both volumes. To the best of my understanding, about fifty copies of the book were printed. I firmly believe that Grandfather also wrote a second volume (tomo 2), although it was apparently never printed. Who knows what happened to it or whether it still exists. I hope that some day the manuscript will be found and published.

Because of my special relationship with my grandfather and because I am the last living member of his family who knew him personally, it has naturally fallen to me to translate his memoirs. I believe that the recollections of this remarkable man should be made available to the widest audience possible. Having studied both Spanish and English and having done considerable translation work for oil companies, radio and television stations, newspapers, and government agencies, I felt confident enough to undertake the task. Therefore, when Thomas H. Kreneck of Texas A&M University–Corpus Christi asked me to do the translation, I readily accepted the challenge, feeling that the endeavor would be like any another project. I must admit, however, that my grandfather's Spanish from the 1800s varies greatly from what I know, so periodically I had to turn to dictionaries and other sources to determine his precise meaning. Regardless of the magnitude of this challenge, I wish to

Luis Gonzaga Gómez and Brígida Cano Gómez. Courtesy of Guadalupe Valdez Jr., Special Collections and Archives, Mary and Jeff Bell Library, Texas A&M University–Corpus Christi.

thank Thomas Kreneck for initiating this effort and expending so many hours in coordinating the project.

To ensure the clarity of my grandfather's memoirs, I have at times translated his words literally, while at other times I have rendered them figuratively. Such is the art of translating. In the editorial process, we have also at times had to break extremely long paragraphs and to correct or include punctuation when absolutely necessary. My tendency, however, has been to avoid tampering with the original prose. Because translation is an art, it is in part subjective. I have been guided by the desire to balance Grandfather's exact words with his message, always attempting to remain true to what he wanted to say, as best as I could determine it. When necessary I have added a translator's note at the bottom of the page. When I felt it best to leave a Spanish word or phrase in the body of the text, I have inserted my brief translation of that word or phrase in brackets.

I have also used brackets where I believed that additional wording was necessary or when my grandfather may have misspelled or rendered incorrectly an English surname, which occurs mainly in chapter 7. In the case of the Stafford couple, with whom Grandfather had his most memorable contact, I have

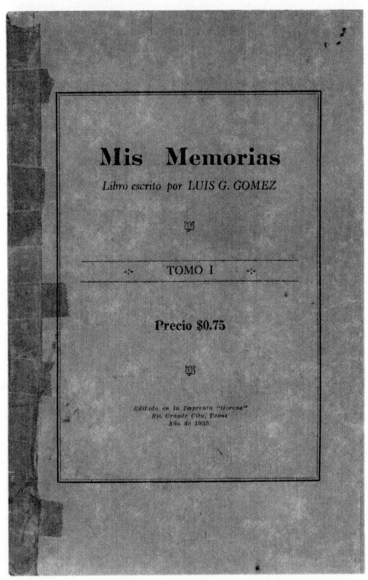

Cover of an original edition of Luis G. Gómez, *Mis Memorias* (Rio Grande City, 1935). Special Collections and Archives, Mary and Jeff Bell Library, Texas A&M University–Corpus Christi.

altered his spelling from "Staford" to "Stafford," again conforming to what I believe is more correct. For clarity, we have also at times added quotation marks around spoken words. These additional quotation marks occur primarily in chapters 6 and 7. Parentheses occur in the text only when they are present in the original Spanish version. For those readers who want to pursue the precise wording or issues that my grandfather addresses, I would urge them to consult a copy of the Spanish version of *Mis Memorias* at A&M–Corpus Christi.

My thanks go to Javier Villarreal for smoothing out my translation. I appreciate the manner in which he has retained the tone of my translation yet made the final product flow. I also appreciate his personal interest in my grandfather's story, which no doubt accounts for the many additional hours he spent on the translation.

I hope that our finished product does justice to the message that Luis G. Gómez wished to convey. If so, the experiences that took place long ago and his memory, which is dear to me, will be handed down to future generations.

Corpus Christi, Texas
April 28, 2005

NOTES

1. From the original chapter 5, 100.
2. From the original chapter 7, 117–18.

MIS MEMORIAS

(MY MEMORIES)

BY LUIS G. GÓMEZ

VOLUME I

PRICE $ .75

PRINTED BY GORENA PRESS

RIO GRANDE CITY, TEXAS

YEAR 1935

Prologue

T HIS HUMBLE BOOK, which I present for the consideration of the public who loves to read, has been composed
with the sole idea of serving as a means of entertainment.
There is no doubt that these readings, if read with patience,
will be of great help to the young. They will find in *Mis Memorias* beautiful examples of filial obedience, which, if imitated,
would make parents striving to attain their children's good fortune very happy.

I have divided this work into two parts because of unavoid-
able circumstances. The first part of my book includes the most
notable incidents of the first years of my youth, which were
printed in my soul with indelible characters and which will, in
my humble opinion, not lack in interest and entertainment. In
the pages of this first volume, the reader will find real-life experiences that may appear to be tall tales. However, as a faithful, sincere man, I assure you that all of the incidents portrayed
were actual happenings.

For the second volume I have reserved some other celebrated, entertaining incidents in which real-life experiences of
my humble story will be woven with those of many other people
of Rio Grande City and surrounding towns. These individuals
have honored me with their sincere friendship to this day. I am
certain that my amiable readers who reside in this region know
many if not all of these people, a reason they should be on the
lookout for the second volume coming out soon and should ac-
quire it to complete the entire work.[1]

The style that I have used to write this book is simple and
comprehensible in the hope of avoiding tiresome reading. I
know my writing has many defects and errors, but I am count-

ing on the amiable public who do me the honor of reading it to excuse me, given the enormous sacrifices incurred in its publication.

Respectfully the author,
Luis G. Gómez
Rio Grande City, Texas
October 1935

NOTES

1. This second volume was never published, nor has its manuscript been located.

Contents

Chapter 1

My Pilgrimage in Texas

*Where the Reader May See the Ability of a Swindler
and Other Actions That Are Worthwhile Reading*

HAVING TO IMMIGRATE into the United States somewhere around 1884, I left my country, México, and crossed the Rio Grande in a ferryboat, the only means of transportation available in those days to the beautiful, florescent state of Texas. This crossing took place on June 14, 1884, with only one goal in mind: to work and accumulate a fortune if at all possible. I had determined beforehand to go to Corpus Christi and from there to proceed into the interior of the state. I worked at different places until by chance I met Mr. Eleodoro Tamez, a native of China, Nuevo León, México, an honorable man and a tireless worker, besides being very intelligent. Because of his kind and sincere disposition, a great sympathy for him grew in me since we were working companions and worked for a sound company that at the time was building several miles of fences. Mr. Tamez was the *mayordomo* [foreman] of a *cuadrilla* [crew] of twenty-five men. The company's custom at that time was to pay on a monthly basis and give the foreman or commissioned person all the money needed to pay each worker. Mr. Tamez was overloaded with work, so he needed someone who knew about numbers and could help at the *comisaria* [in this case, apparently the supply headquarters, including payroll]. The new person would be in charge of keeping precise accounts on payments made to the workers. This is when Mr. Eleodoro hired me to work as a bookkeeper, and indeed I did do the job to the satisfaction of both [the workers and Mr. Tamez].

Don Eleodoro gained confidence in and affection toward me, for which I will be grateful as long as I live, and may this be of encouragement to his surviving family members. Mr. Tamez passed away eight years ago, leaving his second wife and many children, the majority of them males, residing in San Benito, Texas. A virtuous woman, Paulita Tamez, daughter of Mr. Eleodoro (my unforgettable deceased friend), is my daughter-in-law. She married my son, Mr. Apolonio Gómez, and they are now residents of Kingsville, Texas.

But let us continue with the story: We were saying that the simple task of helping Mr. Tamez as a *comisario* was enough for him to invite me to form an alliance with him, as he used to say, or a company, as we now call it. The plan was to move toward Central Texas once our job was done, to get contracts clearing land and to make cords of wood, which were well paid at that time—and that's what we did. We moved to Central Texas after having visited Victoria, Texas, where we did our first job under the name of "Tamez-Gómez and Co." in 1888. Next we pushed forward to Cuero, Texas, where my associate obtained a job in the construction of the bridge across the Guadalupe River, which serves as a means of communication between Cuero and Goliad. My job was to pay the workers, of whom there were never fewer than fifty men, and every week we would share our profits. We would keep a book where our entries were recorded, and I was the acting treasurer. When we finished the job, which lasted about ninety days, we moved on. In February 1889 we joined a railroad company that began laying a railroad line from San Antonio to Kenedy, Texas, proceeding toward Houston and passing through well-known towns like Runge, Yorktown, Cuero, Yoakum, Sweet Home, Hallettsville, and other places. The name of the company was the Aransas Pass Company, and it would pay every ninety days. We worked under this system for more than a year until one day an individual, one of the workers, started reneging and complaining, "It was impossible to live without money." He would say this because the news had spread and there was a lot of concern that the company was not going to pay what was owed to us. These rumors were overheard by a bank in Wallis, Texas, that offered to pay seventy-five cents for every dollar to

Mexican workers laying railroad track in South Texas, early 1900s.
Courtesy of the Hidalgo County Historical Museum.

everyone who owned "check-times," or promissory notes, from
the company.[1] The complainant who gave out the first sign of
alarm was a wily fox who made the rest of us feel like innocent
lambs. The American financiers knew this sharp character and
used him as a talebearer. They told him to spread this rumor
throughout the camp and to alarm everyone, making us easy
prey for exploitation.

Thinking that the company would not pay us but the bank
would pay seventy-five cents on the dollar, we would all rush to
the bank, a normal thing to do, but that was a trick to defraud
us. That is why the wily fox griped deceitfully and lamented
bitterly to reinforce his misleading information. This crooked
character knew it all; he was the camp's mail carrier, running
mail and gossip at his convenience. Luckily the American
money changers spread this rumor through him in the belief
that they alone were going to benefit from this deal, but they
were mistaken.

As I was saying, that infernal swindler grumbled so much
that he even said that he could not care less, that he was going
to cash in his promissory notes for seventy-five cents, which
was good money, and that it would be worse if the company
kept it all, even if it meant a loss to the others. He added that

he was not as stupid as many thought he was. Finally he said to us, "That's the way it is, friends and companions, if you desire to sell your earnings, all you have to do is sign your promissory notes, and I will personally take them and collect your money, which I will place in your hands. Tonight I will warn all the men who can be decisive so we can foil the company's plot."

Thunder! No one escaped the trap. More than fifty men signed the required forms, and not one of them was worth less than $75. Five Americans also fell in, including the plowman with $150. This evil scoundrel knew that the Galveston–El Paso train would allow him enough time to escape with $4,000 or more and be in México by daybreak singing "La Golondrina" without any danger to himself.[2]

We waited in vain all day long but did not begin to lose trust until late that evening. Some thought that something bad might have happened to him but that he would be back at work early in the morning. It was not until the following morning that we found out about that rascal's strategy. We were even left without any way to beg him, for we knew that the train carrying the bandit and the money would arrive at El Paso at 10 P.M. At this time we were very comfortable *comiendo anseras* [literally, "eating geese," which connotes a stimulant that avoids indigestion when things go wrong. In other words, they were helpless in the situation].

The plowman promised to kill him if he saw him, but the swindler would not be affected by such threats because he was way out of danger. The anger did not last long, for we all started commenting to one another, and soon afterward it became a big joke throughout the camp. I was one of the fortunate ones because, in addition to my $2 a day in wages, I was also the camp's barber, which netted me $20 a week. This money I kept with the foreman because his wife was the cashier. This arrangement enabled me not to end up broke from the premeditated trickery by the noted thief, whose mischief we did not even smell.

Having lost everything, Mr. Tamez insisted that we abandon this job since we were not profiting from it since that miserable rascal stole from us the little we had saved. At the end of the month we agreed to leave our employment with the railroad company, but not before I collected my money from the foreman. My savings amounted to $375, to be paid God only knew when because the company had already missed several installments. That is why the workers were unhappy. And it was the same reason the thief had been able to take advantage of us through a scheme that none of us was able to foresee.

As we left, the foreman told us that he was sure the company would pay everything owed to the workers, especially now that the Aransas Company was being sold to the F. C. A. Pass, where it was stipulated in the buy-sell contract that all personnel who were owed would be paid. When the foreman gave me the information, I was impressed with his optimism. At the same time, he asked me to contact him as soon as we settled somewhere so that he could keep us informed on the buy-sell contract results. This we did after settling in the little town of Yoakum, Texas, La Vaca County. The year was 1890.

The Tamez-Gómez Company returned to its interrupted tasks, and with great enthusiasm we again started our primitive system as contractors, which gave us such lucrative and steady results that we never worried about the railroad companies in the least. Although I did write the foreman once, he did not answer. It did not bother me because by then the sun was shining on our faces, and our financial situation was getting better day by day.

All was well. However, I do not want to overlook the fact that that my associate and intimate friend, although a beautiful person and a loyal and sincere friend, was not without a weak spot. In other words, as we normally say, he possessed some defects that I considered degrading. He loved women, and if he liked one, he squandered all of his money to the point of bankruptcy, as Americans would say. Since I was the bookkeeper, I would often caution him that if he did not abstain from "feeding the birds," he would soon be flat broke. "Oh, don't worry over such a trifling thing," he would answer jokingly. "The reason you worry is that you have not reached your peak of happiness. Besides, what is man on earth for? Man has to accomplish his mission. How are we to boast of our name, which the Creator gave us, that powerful title of 'man'? In what other manner can we fulfill our mission if it is not by seeking our happiness, which is the greatest ambition that man feels? Oh, how sublime is women's companionship," he would continue saying. Although many years have passed, I still vividly remember his observations. "Women," he would continue, "regardless of their position or their race, have an identical manner of making a man happy." I swear, my fellow readers, that when that man would finish speaking in those terms, I was not sure that I could sustain a spiritual confession without being condemned— and that is how we enjoyed many a hilarious pastime.

One day my friend received a letter from México and, after reading it, told me with much happiness, "I must return to my birth land. You see, my fiancée, whom I left back home when I started my venture about five years ago, is waiting for me still as pure as a white flower of Jericho, according to my parents. When I left her she was only a little girl. She was a beautiful creature who was barely thirteen years old. Her respectable parents and mine were always in accord that I would marry her, but you see I did not deem it convenient and decided instead to wait one or two years, time that I would use to make money and then marry my promised one when it was convenient. As you know, it has been impossible for me to save money. Time passes in the middle of adventures and in the hazardous lifestyle I have adopted, including unfortunate incidents like the one we had with the check-times. I had almost forgotten that delicate project [back in Mexico]. Although I thought my noted absence and prolonged silence would cool off her and our families' desires, the situation had developed otherwise. It was something I would never have imagined. Oh, my God, what a wonderful surprise! I believe everything is predetermined by the hand of God, whose guardian angel watches over this saintly woman, whose soul is pure and white and who waits for the man who had promised to marry and to love her forever."

That is the way my friend expressed himself when he received that enchanting missive. This was such a great surprise that he felt as if it had come from the heavens. We immediately prepared ourselves—we agreed to adhere to a rigorous financial plan and save a sum of $200 or $300, an amount he deemed sufficient to go and surrender himself into the embrace of one who patiently waited for him amid the happiness of both families.

However, things are always easier said than done, and we had to wait longer than we had imagined. This is when it was time for me to harangue my friend in the following terms: "If you had controlled yourself by not giving yourself to the misleading silk enchantments, the attractive laces, the fragrant perfumes of so many flowers and throwing your money away, you would now have enough money to make your trip to your homeland and your adorable sweetheart. But now it is too late, and only God knows if you will be successful in your pilgrimage in this strange land." "Do not be so old-fashioned," he answered me good-naturedly. "You sound like a patriarch. If things do not have a remedy, you leave them as they are without making a commotion." This is how our discussion ended—as a joke.

We were experiencing a crisis because of a serious dry spell that prevailed throughout the country. This is when an American gentleman who resided some fifteen miles north of Yoakum offered us a job and wanted to talk to one of us, a member of the Tamez-Gómez Company. Immediately we sought a means to communicate with Mr. Manning, the gentleman who was interested in us.

A RARE COINCIDENCE

It so happened at the same time that we were discussing the offer that a gentleman from town, a friend of ours whose name was Francisco Del Bosque, requested that we go and ask—on behalf of his son—for the hand in marriage of a local girl. It just so happened that this young lady resided with her family in the same town where Mr. Manning lived—the same person we wanted to talk to. We got together to discuss the new issue, and Mr. Tamez was commissioned to preside over the committee asking for the hand in marriage of the designated young lady, but my friend excused himself, stating eloquently that he could not speak English. Since we wished to take advantage of the opportunity to also speak to the American, the position of leader was passed to me. That is to say, both projects would be my responsibility: asking the parents for the hand in marriage of the young woman, Constanza Torres, for the young man, Del Bosque, and talking to Mr. Louis Manning about his job. I gladly accepted both commissions, and we set the date and time when we would begin our trip. In gratitude Mr. Del Bosque promised to sponsor the *mueble* [carriage] that was to transport us on our expedition. When I say a mueble, I mean a "carriage" because in those years the only means of transportation involved the use of a horse to pull a carriage. We had not heard about automobiles yet, since the incidents I am relating occurred about the end of the year 1890.

At last we began our well-planned trip at 8 A.M. on the day agreed. We arrived at the little town of Sweet Home, which was our destination, around 11:30 A.M. on the same morning in an elegant carriage pulled by a team of beautiful sorrel-colored horses owned by Mr. Del Bosque Sr. We had agreed beforehand to ask for the precious hand of Miss Torres. If luck was kind, that hand could eventually belong to the interested young man: Mr. Del Bosque Jr. Miss Constanza was such a beautiful young lady she could easily be compared to one of Job's daughters as described in our sacred scriptures. We had agreed to arrive at their home at 1 P.M. or right after lunch. Miss Torres was already aware of our objective. Her suitor had made sure she knew of all of his plans beforehand.

Young Mr. Del Bosque was an exceptional man, very sensitive and quite handsome and quite a celebrity in having love affairs in that territory. This young man was of mixed families. His mother was *criolla* [someone of Spanish blood but born in the New World]. She had been born in Bexar County. His father, don Francisco Del Bosque, was a Spaniard born in Barcelona, Spain, and who had lived in this country since Texas was a republic. Texas was sold thereafter under the Treaty of Guadalupe Hidalgo. According to that treaty, México would lose not only Texas but also New Mexico and Arizona, receiving five million dollars in return.[3]

The cowardice and lack of patriotism by our government [México] from that time caused the loss of this precious land and its inhabitants, among them the Del Bosque family. This family could read and write and speak the English language with admirable perfection, but they chewed Spanish in an imperfect manner. The Torres family was also of mixed racial background. Mr. Máximo Torres, the father, was the son of Mr.

Gustavo Torres, a native of Cuatro Ciénegas, Coahuila, México. They lived in their native state when the American intervention occurred, which resulted in the separation of our fertile and productive state—a land that we appreciated like a precious jewel and whose irreparable loss pained us.[4] This information was shared with us by Mr. Torres, Constanza's father, while under the quiet ceiling of their humble home. Mr. Torres also told me other interesting incidents, including a very pleasant story about his wife, Mrs. Gertrudis Bravo. Tulitas, as she was kindly called within the immediate family, was a direct descendant of the heroic Bravo family of México. Her grandfather had been Mr. Leonardo Bravo, a true liberal insurgent and patriot whose history we all know and who was religiously respected.[5]

Mr. Leonardo Bravo was executed by the Spaniards, and the news reached the ears of his son, Mr. Nicolás Bravo, along with the order to execute three hundred Spaniards he had as prisoners. The order came from General Morelos, who was outraged by the execution of the hero.[6] However, Mr. Nicolás Bravo did not execute his prisoners but instead clothed them and pardoned them the following day.

This incident shows the noble heart of this insurgent general. It was one of the brightest and best-known acts in that war, in which Mexicans fought for their ideals but were pursued and annihilated like wild beasts. The Bravo name will forever live throughout the times. It will be an honor for México, and no one could deny what Mr. Nicolás Bravo was during his time—a flaming torch who would light the path toward Mexican independence, which sooner or later would definitely be won—and the arduous sacrifices made by their illustrious sons, who gave their lives and blood for their beloved México, would not have been in vain. Those heroes will shine like first-magnitude stars in the American sky. They are the ones who opened the doors so that México could enter the great alliance of free nations on earth.

Dear readers, just imagine, doña Tulita belonged to this lineage! When her husband made those verifiable statements, which I deeply appreciated, a great inexpressible satisfaction showed on her face. Miss Constanza was a dignified descendent of her ancestors. Her heart was noble, and she was a very beautiful young lady. Her skin was a pink-white color, and her hair curly and dark black. Her eyes were very penetrating, and her height average; [she was] only nineteen and a half years old and very communicative and frank.

When I was at her home in my role as one of the ones commissioned to ask for her hand in marriage, she was present. Every so often she would excuse herself because her Spanish was very limited and she could not express herself as she would have liked, or at least like her father or the rest of us. Meanwhile she told me she was going to study her language so she could speak it with perfection, as she had promised to "her Frank," as she called her fiancé. However, I must admit that when English was spoken, we were the ones who had to excuse ourselves because our English was very defective.

The time was passing quickly, and it was time for our departure, but we could not take our leave without asking a thousand pardons as we are accustomed to doing when a commission of this nature is performed. You see, these things encompass many mysteries that are the roots of the formation of a human family. Mr. and Mrs. Torres answered that there was no need to ask to be excused, especially when it was the parents' responsibility to be courteous to the members of a commission dealing with such delicate matters. Mrs. Torres told me with assurance that all parents were obligated to see to the welfare of their children, and most of all they should ensure the purification of the race. "In this case," Mrs. Torres continued, "we are entirely satisfied and happy by Mr. Del Bosque's request communicated by you, to whom we are very grateful. You see, in reality the Del Bosque family is an exemplary family that we esteem within our social circle. I believe our daughter has been very wise and above all fortunate in her selection. I am sure that with her proposed companion Constancita has ensured her happiness forever."

We left with such a pronounced, warm good-bye that if Mr. Tamez had led the commission he would have not wanted to depart so soon from the company of such amiable people. As we were leaving, Mr. Torres told us again to notify the groom's family and the interested young man that their answer would be forthcoming within eight days.

We left and proceeded to town, where we went in different directions to take care of our own pending commitments. I went directly to Mr. Manning's house. My visit there was unfruitful since Mr. Manning had, according to his wife, gone to see us about the job in question but had missed us on his way there. Of course, I assumed Mr. Tamez had had an opportunity to talk to him. We had agreed to meet at the railroad station. The understanding was that whoever arrived first would wait for the others in order to arrange our return trip to Yoakum, our final destination.

Another Unusual Incident

I was the first one to reach our meeting place, so I sat on a bench to rest and wait, when I suddenly noticed that the passenger train was about to drop off the mailbag and pick up the outgoing one. At the same time I observed many passengers looking out the windows, and I clearly heard my name being called and the voice also saying, "let's go get our pay. The payroll coach has been in Houston for the last three days. All those who are owed and bring their worked time receipts are being paid." The one who was calling to me was a good friend of mine, Desiderio Pérez, who came to the door to help me get on board. But it was too late. The train was already traveling too fast, and I was unable to climb on. Still, Desiderio acted with great ability. He ran back through the coach's aisles, and when he got to the last one he threw me a newspaper that explained about the payroll coach.

Almost simultaneously my companions arrived, and they found me *con un volcan en la cabeza* [literally, with a volcano in my head, or very excited]. In a few words I made them aware of what was happening, and one of them asked whether I had my work-time receipts with me, and I answered yes. I told him I had a $375 check that was not paid when I left the railroad. I further added that I had just read in the newspaper that the following day was the last day of payments because the company had made the announcement thirty days before and that whoever was not there by the deadline would forever lose the right to be paid. The announcement would protect the company from further claims. After all, they had publicly announced what the company had intended to do, and it would be the creditors' responsibility to be there at the proper time.

My friends, just imagine the difficult situation I was in! However, there was still the hope that the company would allow the employees three days in which to come and collect their wages. However, these rights were always in doubt when the employees were Mexicans. I was distressed when I remembered that every afternoon a freight train would pass by that place. I thought if I could board it that night, I could easily be in Houston by sunrise and cash the checks, which were in my coat pocket inside a little wallet that I always carried when I was on a trip.

My friends and I began to discuss my idea of boarding the freight train at dusk. The train would always stop for water about half a mile from the station, and that would be the proper place to board because it was quite dark and no one lived close by. We all agreed that would be the right location to do what I had proposed. Having agreed on this plan, they returned to Yoakum, and I went out to explore the boarding place to avoid missing such an opportunity. It had to be done. After sharing my plan with my friend Tamez, who was well informed of whatever happened to me, I would return within two or three days. This, of course, if God so willed it. As I have mentioned before, all of my friends returned to their own situations in a very happy mood. They were properly instructed on the answer they would convey to the Del Bosque family in reference to the message sent by the Torres family regarding the hand in marriage of Miss Constanza.

As I said before, I proceeded to inspect the boarding area. Soon I found a place that was ideal. After I had found a good spot in which to hide, I rested and read the newspaper, confident there was nothing else to do until the arrival of the train that would take me to my destination. I had plenty of time to spare. I could read or even sleep if I so desired. It was only 4:00, and the train would not come by until 6:30. By that time it would be dark enough for me to board the train. I could also daydream for two and a half hours about castles in the air. Moreover, why not? I was going to be rich! The 375 *getones* [a slang term for dollars such as "smackeroos" or "bucks"] that I carried in my pocket in check-times were beginning to squirm like a reptile after winter when it begins to come out of hibernation and look for the summer sun to get warm.

After I made myself comfortable, the first thing I did was to review my valuable papers, examining them meticulously to see whether everything was intact. I checked for issued dates on them and how long I had had them in my possession, and I found out to my surprise that I had kept them in my pocket for a year. They were issued on December 10, 1889, and this was December 1890. Thereafter I began to calculate what I could buy with the treasure. I was thinking of buying a good-quality suit and a cheaper one for daily use; a pair of wool shirts, plenty of underwear, dress shirts, ties, and so on. Well, to make a long story short, I will tell you that, about thirty minutes after I arrived at my hiding place, I had already spent a hundred dollars or more, and it still seemed like a trifle.

I believe I fell asleep because I dreamed I was pushing into the interior of a strange country. I awoke about 5, and after becoming aware of what I was doing in that place, I exclaimed "Oh, my God!" and it was so loud I was afraid people had heard me in Yoakum. After that I began to laugh so loud I thought I had become demented. I immediately got up and started to walk along the railroad so as not to create suspicion. After that I began to think about what had occurred to me, and I could not keep from laughing, but this time it was a different kind of laugh from what I had experienced moments before. No wonder some people say that money talks. Well, all I can say is that it made me talk and laugh aloud. Moments later I felt hungry and went as far as the nearby town of Sweet Home to have supper. I wanted to be prepared for the long trip that would last all night long and dawn in Houston, my golden dream. However, as the old saying goes, "Man proposes but God disposes." I did not arrive at dawn as planned. You will see why, my dear readers, as I will relate later.

At last the time approached, the train arrived, and I boarded it without any difficulty. That long steel serpent began to move, slowly at first, then faster and faster until reaching a velocity of thirty-five miles an hour. The ancient adages possess an eminent philosophy, and whoever wrote them were indeed geniuses of the truth. At this point in my story I remember an old adage that if my mind does not deceive me says, "An adventure without vicissitudes is not honorable," and indeed if my adventure had been without misfortune it would have been worthless. And I say this because here comes the best part.

What had to happen, happened. We had traveled barely an hour when, oh, my God! The damned brakeman, who was a quadroon about six feet tall and weighing about 250 pounds caught up with me. Based on my judgment, he was bigger than a man but too small to be an elephant, and immediately without a second look he shouted in English, "Say, hombre, you get off this train!" I begged him not to throw me off. I told him that I was not a hobo, but rather I was a dignified individual to whom the company owed wages and that I was on my way to collect them. I explained to him that the company representatives were in Houston, and it was essential for me to be there at dawn. I said that this was the last day they would pay and tried to show him my documents. But he answered in English, "I do not care, you see," and turned around and left.

We had moved for about five more minutes when I noticed the train was beginning to slow down, and I felt it was because they were going to throw me off. I also noted we were passing a pronounced curve as I could see the locomotive at the front end. Unexpectedly the damned old African emerged at the other end of the platform wagon I was riding on and threatened me by saying in English, "Jump out or I shoot," while wrapping his big hand around a pistol just as big. I could see it very well by the light of the lantern, and it was loaded with several slightly yellow-colored rounds about three inches long.

At that moment I thought this was an opportunity to save myself. The train was moving slowly, and I jumped off quickly to avoid things turning from bad to worse. I also thought about climbing onto the caboose, where I was sure some Anglo would be glad to take me to my destination after I explained my case to him. However, the darkness of the night, coupled with the unfamiliarity of the terrain and the faster speed of the train, spoiled my plans. I damned that quadruped for his wicked behavior, thinking he must not be a Christian.

Finding myself in that predicament, I asked myself, what should I do? Suddenly I thought about how far we had traveled, about the little town of Subin [Sublime], which had been passed, and about that curve I previously mentioned. It was near the plains along the Colorado River, and not far away was a small way station. I thought if my luck held, I could persuade the manager to telephone Houston to get assurance my pay would be there even if at a discount. I also thought about selling my check-times at Eagle Lake, which was just on the other side of the Colorado River. Of course, I had to have help from someone who would take me that same day. That would comfort me enough. With that in mind I felt better and pushed on all night with a lot of faith and renewed hope.

At dawn, as soon as I was able to distinguish objects, I found myself in the middle of that immense wide-open space where not even a single shrub was to be seen—not even a bird was flying. I felt my soul sadden at seeing such a wide-open space all alone and desolate where it appeared no human being had set foot. I sat down to rest for the first time since I had left the flatcar. It must have been 10 at night. Just imagine it had already dawned! After having meditated while sitting there, I realized I had made a stupid decision in boarding that freight train clandestinely. It was well known that no one was allowed to board the train, but the overpowering need pushed me into doing it on the sly. At that time I also had difficulty with my English, and I assure you that anyone listening to my English would get a stomachache. At the same time, I thought that if I had shown the conductor my papers, it was possible my proposal might have been realized, but all these ideas came too late.

Then I began to reflect upon what that infernal Negro behind that monstrous pistol I saw with the light of the lantern had done to me that extremely dark night. I figured it was two feet long, and the yellow-colored rounds that were shining brightly in the womb of that enormous two-barrel gun looked like lit ovens that were ready to spew fire. Now tell me, dear readers, who would not have been scared in front of that tall Negro, the big pistol, and the described rounds? I was more than flying when I jumped into the precipice with the possibility of turning into a tortilla against those embankments. By the time I finished turning around in midair, the train had already passed me, and I was about fifty feet away from the rail, so it was too late for me to jump onto the caboose. I thought of getting even with that black panther man by doing what the plowman had promised to do with the swindler who stole our money and escaped to México. However, the plowman never saw that Mexican again. But in my case, although briefly, I did meet with that infamous brakeman who made me roll into that abyss. When I saw him, I thought about getting even with him. However, let us continue with our story, and we will talk about this heartless mulatto later.

The morning was cold and gloomy, and as the day progressed, the bushes and shrubs were becoming much clearer. Suddenly I saw at a distance a white thing that I thought was a sand dune, but later I discarded that idea because I noted the terrain was solid and fertile. The section house I was looking for was not far from the railroad. I got up from where I was sitting. I had already rested enough but was thirsty because I had not eaten or drunk anything since I had eaten supper at Sweet Home the day before, and it was already 7 in the morning of the following day. I pushed on hard, and as I walked, I could see more clearly that what I had thought was a sand dune was a building constructed not far from the railroad. I immediately set my sights in that direction. Now I could see in that part of the terrain cattle grazing in the pasture. The pasture was abundant, and the cattle were of good breed with mainly white faces. They all looked well fed, which indicated that the owner must be well to do. Now I could clearly see the dwelling, and as I was nearing it, I thought I would talk to the owner, and it was sooner than later that I got my wish.

Now we have arrived at one of the most important highlights of my true story. As I got closer, I noticed it was a beautiful country home constructed with much love and possessing all the accouterments. It had a viewing area toward the sunrise and long wide corridors, magnificent barnyards, and granaries with a large henhouse where more than two hundred of the same type of colored chickens were seen. They all were of a breed called "Rhode Island Red" and reflected the sunlight, which was beginning to shine. To be truthful, I had never seen such an

　　　　　　　　MIS MEMORIAS (MY MEMORIES)

enchanting view. It was wonderful to see such a beautiful flock spread out over an extra clean and well-manicured patio. There was nothing left to ask for.

Two people were sitting at the end of the corridor facing the sunrise. One of them was a white person, and the other one was black. The distance from the house to the railroad was about two hundred feet, and this building and all of the surrounding structures were within a fence that was about three and a half feet high and made of red picket material. This decor contrasted beautifully with the recently painted big white house with lemon-green trimmings. It was an enchanting scene.

But let us continue with our story. I mentioned there were two people sitting on the corridor facing east, one white and the other black. Immediately I resolved to ask the people if the station house I was looking for was not far from here. I left the track I was walking on, and I went to the house. I coughed lightly and refitted my coat, which was buttoned up because of the slightly chilly morning, and I began to think of English phrases that would be proper for the occasion. The gate was unlocked. I stopped in front of the gate without forcing my way in. I greeted the people after I took my hat off with my left hand, and, lightly extending my right hand, I offered a "buenos días." It was so unpretentious I even liked it myself. These two women were both married. The white woman was a young lady about twenty years old at most. The black one was about forty-five years old. The white lady was breastfeeding about a two-month-old child. The black lady, who was at her side, was churning butter in a clay butter maker that was very popular in those days among the North American families. When the Anglo lady saw me, she got up from her chair so fast I thought she had a spring under her. She answered me in English, "Good morning." I immediately spoke to her in Spanish and asked for the man of the house. She answered in English that he had just left a moment ago, but she was sure he would return soon. I learned that this lady understood some Spanish because I would address her in Spanish, and she would answer in English. Little by little, we became more familiar with each other, and she asked whether I had an urgent matter to discuss with her husband and, if so, to come in and wait inside. I realized she was a good-natured woman who deserved consideration and respect from everyone she knew.

As she demonstrated great interest in my motive in coming to her house, I began to explain, partly in broken English and partly in Spanish, what I wished. She understood me quite well. Showing her my check-times, I explained to her my urgent desire to go to Houston this very day, and she kindly replied that I should wait for her husband, who would soon return. In front of the house there was a pile of wood and tree trunks of century plants that had been cut with a swing saw. Instead of being idle and disrupting the people in the house, I went out and picked up an ax lying beside the tree trunks and began to split them. From that moment on, I noticed that the mysterious young lady seemed very restless, but I could not imagine the reason for her behavior.

A few hours passed, but I was still determined to split those trunks, which by the way were very tough, when suddenly, when I was busy with my job, the American who owned the ranch and was the husband of the mysterious lady who was previously breastfeeding her baby, who was as red as a shrimp, showed up. The American man, owner of the house, was riding a proud black horse with sharp movements and sporting a magnificent, brand-new saddle. It was very beautiful. It must have been very expensive. He was a gentleman of about fifty years of age with a moustache and gray hair. He was wearing a white winged hat cocked to the right and almost covering his right eye. He was sitting more to the riding side, according to cowboy practice. He had a red handkerchief around his neck with the ends on his shoulders. He got to where I was and asked me in English, "Chopping wood are you?" "Yes, sir," I answered in Spanish. Meanwhile, the mysterious young woman was standing by the corridor signaling to her husband to come to her. She urgently wanted to talk to him even before he dismounted. He understood his wife's urgency and went to her without stopping. She came close to him and spoke in his ear for about two minutes.

At this moment I was doing two jobs at the same time: chopping wood and trying to observe their discussion. I had forgotten to mention that in front of the corridor was a beautiful hackberry tree, also known as an umbrella tree, and on that tree was a nail where my coat was hanging with my personal records in it. These were the same records I had previously shared with the mysterious lady. I suppose, dear readers, that you may wonder why I continue referring to that lady as mysterious. You may think I do not have any reason to describe her as such, but I do have my reason. You see, when I arrived at their place, I noticed a certain interest mixed with restlessness in addition to her urgent secretive message to her husband. Besides, she showed great curiosity when she read my personal records. Finally, there were other details that seemed enigmatic to me.

After he stopped talking with his wife, the American got off his horse, pulled it by the bridle, and tied it at the same place where I had hung my coat. Then he proceeded to the home's corridor, dragging his spurs and making noise with his chaps. He quickly sat down in the same rocking chair where his wife had been breastfeeding her baby shrimp. As soon as he sat down, he beckoned to me to come near him, and he exclaimed in Spanish, "Hombre, venga para acá" [Man, come here].

I promptly put down the ax and was happy to do so because the century-plant wood was very tough to cut and had left me short of breath. I walked toward him, and he said in Spanish, "Pase usted" while pointing to a chair next to him and motioning to me to sit there. But the lady, who was never motionless, suggested it would be better to come in and sit at the dining table to discuss whatever we wished because breakfast was ready.

We entered the dining room: He entered first and I followed him. He sat at the head of the table and motioned to me to sit to his left. His wife sat to his right, facing me. She then let us know she had already had her breakfast and then asked me to excuse her for not having a full breakfast but to make myself at home. I sincerely thanked her for her excellent manners as she herself served me a huge cup of smoking, aromatic coffee that, after working so hard chopping wood, tasted like a million dollars. She continued asking me to help myself to what was on the table such as ham, potatoes, gravy, butter, syrup, and other things there. But I attacked the butter and syrup, which disappeared beautifully because in all honesty I was truly hungry, and the food was so good that I kept on eating.

Let us pause for a moment to consider the graceful attention that had been shown me by my unique protector, who without doubt had been sent by heaven. Let us focus on the wishes of the man of the house, who wanted to know the whole story that I had shared with his wife. I wanted to cooperate fully, but I had great difficulty in expressing myself in English, and I told him so. However, he asked me to relate it in the manner I had explained it to his wife and said that if he could not understand me, he would ask his wife for help.

Well, I began from way back when I started working for the Aransas Pass Company. Then he said he knew the background of that company but to continue with what had happened to me lately. I told him the company had promised to pay us with check-times, which we received, but those documents were never converted into cash. At that moment he interrupted me by saying in Spanish, "Mi esposa me dijo que usted trae consigo esos papeles. Yo desearía verlos" [My wife told me that you have some papers. I would like to see them]. I answered that I would be glad to show them to him. Then I started to get up to go get them since they were in my coat pocket hanging on the umbrella tree, but just then the petite lady got up as fast as the wind (she was short and red faced, something that I failed to mention). She said, "No se moleste usted. Acabe su almuerzo" [Do not bother. Finish your breakfast.], and she darted outside to get my wallet, which was in the front pocket of my coat.

She got the papers and brought them over to us. When she was in front of me, she handed me the little book. I kindly thanked her and immediately passed the papers over to the American gentleman. He quickly looked them over and then handed them to me and said in English, "I see." I then got up, excused myself, and started to walk back to my coat to put the papers away and go back to work cutting those tough century-plant limbs. But no sooner had I returned to my project where the ax was when he said in English, "Say, L. G., come here." I walked back to where he was, and he asked me if I knew how to harness a team of horses. "Yes, sir," I answered. Then he said, "Good. Go to the barn where the horses are and harness them. Each one of them has their harness on their side since both are in their own stable. After the horses are harnessed, hitch them to the buggy that has the *fuete pinto* [a special colored whip]."

Quickly I went to harness the horses, and while I was doing so, I heard thunderous sounds like furniture being turned upside down or thrown against each other. All of this was very mysterious. During the commotion in the house, the black woman was seen running from one side to the other, and then I saw her going toward the chicken coop carrying a white aluminum bucket in her hand. Dear readers, I cannot describe my feelings at seeing such a disturbance and not knowing what it was all about. It was very difficult for me to untangle this chaotic behavior. Finally I hitched the horses to the buggy, and then I brought it to the door. But I noticed with surprise that the horses were so frisky and eager to get started that for a moment I felt like getting off that buggy, and I would have, had I not had experience as a rancher. Those horses were very vigorous and well rested, doing nothing more than being well fed in their stable.

As I said before, I brought the buggy to the house door and intended to get off, but I heard the American tell me not to get off and to hold on to the reins. Then I saw him come out accompanied by his wife, who appeared to be hanging by his neck as he was walking backward toward me, but she was actually knotting his loose tie. When they separated, I noticed the American was another person. That is, he looked like another person. He was now wearing a nice suit and looked like a distinguished gentleman. His suit was jet black with stripes of silver threads embedded in the cloth; they could barely be seen in the background of that fine suit, which was quite becoming to him. He was wearing an extremely white shirt made out of fine linen, silk socks, and expensive charcoal-black shoes. His hands were covered with skintight gloves made of fine leather. I noted that around his wrists were black straps made from otter skin with a bright furry trim that looked nice; their laps were secured with a pressed button protruding through a gold-covered eyelet. He was wearing a solid black felt hat cocked slightly to the right. I made all these observations very quickly.

He himself took my coat, which was hanging on the hackberry tree, and laid it over my legs. As he sat down on my left, the black woman suddenly appeared to my right; she was carrying the white aluminum bucket that I had seen her with when I was harnessing the horses. She had filled it with eggs laid by the beautiful sorrel-colored hens I had so admired coming out of the coop at first light that morning. She gave me the bucket, and the American told me to hold it tight. Then I again asked myself if I knew what it all meant—but later on I would know. Meanwhile, let us continue with our story. When he told me to be sure the bucket was well secured, I sensed that something extraordinary was going to happen. Sure enough, he then took the reins and loosened them, and the horses took off at a gallop.

As soon as we departed, I glanced back to see if I could see the mysterious young lady. I was hoping to say good-bye, even if it were only a head nod since my hands were tied up with that bucketful of eggs in midair, making sure they did not get broken. It was very distressing to me not to be able to thank the person who had helped me in so many and noble ways and whose protection I would still enjoy, as my readers will learn in due time. What had happened up to now was only the beginning of what was yet to occur.

When I looked back to see where she was with the intent of saying farewell, I noticed she was blessing the buggy. This reminded me of our own culture, as we are also accustomed to bestowing a blessing when we say farewell to members of the family who are departing, asking God to protect them on their journey. I swear to you that the actions of this mysterious lady really surprised me. I also remember that, when her husband was saying his farewell to her, when picking up my coat, she said to him in perfect English, "Oh, dear, I am almost sure you have time." All of this was still a mystery to me, and I taxed my brain trying to understand it. Finally we left the ranch at such a high speed that it felt like we were flying. Nonetheless, he kept using the whip on the horses.

We took a direction opposite to what I thought was the town of Eagle Lake, traveling in the midst of a dust cloud at breakneck speed. About five miles from the ranch, we went west until we came to a curve that directed us northward. When we got to the center of the curve, the American gentleman gave a questioning look to see where we were in relation to the ranch and whipped the horses to increase their speed—or so I imagined. Then I noticed we were on the Colorado River bridge, where all vehicles pulled by animals traveled. But not even for

Mis Memorias (My Memories)

Passenger train, late 1800s. From James L. Rock and W. I. Smith, *Southern and Western Texas Guide for 1878* (St. Louis: A. H. Granger, 1878), 199.

crossing the bridge did he slow down—this was something that surprised me.

As soon as we were on solid ground again, that curve in the road continued leading us to the next town, which was about five miles away. Again he made another one of his strange looks, which was very perplexing to me. Then he pulled out his watch from his vest pocket, glanced at it, put it back in its place, and continued whipping the horses. Soon after, we could see the houses of the town, and my thoughts began to change.

It must have been about nine o'clock in the morning when we neared the town. He then took the road that would lead us to the railroad station—prodding the horses more and more and, without hesitation, making a sudden stop at the station. He then told me to leave the bucketful of eggs there. Then he gave me the reins, told me to wait, got off the buggy, and ran into the office. Moments later another American without a hat rushed out, carrying a white flag in his hand, and crossed the rails. At this time my man came out with a ticket and a handful of fluttering bills and hurriedly said, "This is a ticket so you can get to Houston in time to collect your pay. This is so you will not arrive broke," and he gave me the ticket and the money.

Then he took the reins and almost pushed me off the buggy so I could catch the train, which was just arriving. I wanted badly to thank him for such a benevolent action, but then he said, "No, no, quick, the train will depart without you." A Negro porter who was on the steps helped me get on board. This was no ordinary train that would go by there at 1:15 and arrive in Houston at 7, just about dark. The train I had just boarded was a special one where the gentlemen who were going to assume ownership of the Aransas Pass Company were passengers. This train was also carrying many new employees and their families the company needed in Houston. There were also many workmen who were owed money by the Aransas Pass Company who knew when the last day of payment was going to be. They had waited until the final day to come and collect their money. Mr. Stafford was the name of the American who brought me, and he and his gracious wife knew about the train that was to go by at that particular time.[7]

It was only then that I finally understood some of the mysterious actions by Mr. Stafford and his wife back at the ranch. They knew the exact hour that train would arrive. They therefore thought that if they hurried, Mr. Stafford could get me there in time to catch it so I could get to Houston to collect my money. It was indeed a noble action from their generous hearts, for which I am and will be grateful as long as I live. You can imagine, my readers, my good fortune when I landed in the hands of such kind people.

There existed a difficult circumstance between these generous people. She was a very religious person. He was not. She was very well educated and enlightened. Later I found out she had a degree in science that she was pleased to have obtained. When I first arrived at her house and showed her all my documents, which was all I had at the time, she understood my predicament and immediately realized she was going to do God's work. But I was very naïve and could not understand why that woman, who was placed in the middle of my worst adversity, extended her protective hand to me. These are mysteries of human life that only our creator can penetrate!

NOTES

1. The term "check-times" seems to equate with the promissory notes the company issued as pay to the workers.

2. "La Golondrina" [The Swallow] was a very popular, sad song in Mexico in the late 1800s and early 1900s. It is a farewell song sung by a gentleman to his ladylove.

3. The United States actually paid Mexico $18,250,000 for the lands ceded by the Treaty of Guadalupe Hidalgo. See Robert A. Calvert and Arnoldo De León, *The History of Texas* (Arlington Heights, Ill.: Harlan Davidson, 1990), 96.

4. What Gómez refers to here as "our fertile and productive state" is Texas under Mexican rule.

5. A noted *hacendado* [landowner] from Chilpanzingo, don Leonardo Bravo was a leader with José María Morelos during the 1810–1821 Mexican independence movement against Spain.

6. Gómez refers here to General José María Morelos.

7. We have altered Gómez's original spelling of this person's name from "Staford" to "Stafford."

Chapter 2

My Arrival in Houston

Where My Check-Times Were Paid with Pure Solid Gold

As soon as I was well situated in that luxurious special train, I meditated on all that had happened to me. It all seemed like a dream or something that I had read in the story of *A Thousand and One Nights*. I remembered that it was only a few hours ago that I was forced to get off that freight train by that cruel African brakeman, and now I was walking very peacefully and happily toward the place of my golden dreams, Houston!

What had really happened? Multiple thoughts danced in my mind and left me stunned and confused: my arrival at the blessed home where my mysterious little woman lived, her uneasiness when she saw all my unpaid receipts, her interest in my plight, and her urging her husband to take me to where I could catch the special train. She created quite a commotion in that house while trying hard to help her husband speedily remove his work clothes, removing his boots, his chaps, his spurs, and whatever else there was to remove. While he was dressing up in his clean shirt and fresh suit, she was shining his shoes, brushing his hat; meanwhile, it was also necessary to harness the team of horses to the buggy. All of those things were running through my mind, and my thoughts were so many that they were crowding one another, causing me to become sentimental and to feel great admiration and gratitude that emerged from the deepest part of my soul. Even the black woman entered my mind as she went hurriedly to the chicken coop to gather that bucketful of eggs—and everything was done because of me! Oh, noble souls, may God bless you! At that moment I was thanking the good Lord with all my heart for having led me to those noble hearts who deserved my admiration and praise! But I felt really sorry that I was beginning to travel away from them and would not have an opportunity to prove to them that I was not an ungrateful man. But at every moment I was getting farther away from them and did not know whether I would ever see them again.

At 1:15 that afternoon the train arrived in Houston. What a pleasure! I was elated that I was finally going to be paid! As I got off the train, a friend of mine, Desiderio Pérez, was already waiting for me. We had worked together for the same company, but he had been ordered to go to San Antonio a few days before that swindler took all our money—the cheat who perhaps arrived in México City early the next morning with four thousand dollars belonging to more than fifty employees. Mysteriously, I escaped the trickery that you readers are already familiar with.

Main Street, Houston, Texas, looking south, late 1880s, the place of Luis Gómez's "golden dreams." Courtesy of the Houston Metropolitan Research Center, Houston Public Library.

From the railroad station, my friend Desiderio and I walked to where the paying car was parked. My friend Pérez entered before I did, and he immediately announced that they were calling out for "Mr. L. G. Gómez, payer for the company for more than two years."

"Mr. Gómez," said the payer, "we have been calling for you for the last three days."

"Yes, sir," I answered, "but it was impossible for me to be here sooner."

"Do you have your paperwork ready?"

"Yes, sir," I answered as I took out all of the documents from my wallet and gave them to him. He took them and spread them out over his account book. Then he opened the safety box, which was to his right, pulled out a canvas bag, and opened it. He then counted out ten ounces of gold coins valued at $20 each (paper money was not in circulation in those days), then ten coins worth $10 each, and ten more coins worth $5 each. Then he gave me $25 in silver, which made a total of $375.

At last, thanks to the helping hand of my mysterious petite woman, I was now a rich man! The payer counted all of the money for me, and then he asked me to please sign his ledger. I signed it, thanked him, and left his office with my friend. At that moment the other people who had been my traveling companions and who also needed to be paid began to arrive. My friend and I then happily departed toward the downtown area of the city with the intent of buying some clothes, bathing, and getting a shave. As soon as we were all tidied up, we were ready to leap into the urban adventures that were abundant throughout the city.

Chapter 3

The Negro Brakeman!

Where You Will See the Effect Caused to Him by Seeing Me When He Least Expected

BEFORE WE VENTURED through the streets of that crowded city, my friend Pérez and I made sure we would have a decent place to stay. After we did that, we went out to visit a family, friends of ours, who lived there in Houston and whom we had previously visited. This family lived on the other side of the bridge not too far from the paying car where I had collected my money. We had already crossed the bridge when, to our surprise, we met up with—whom do you think, dear readers, we met? Well, we met the darn Negro brakeman who had run me off of the cargo train the night before near the town of Sublin [Sublime]. As soon as I saw him, I recognized him, and my guts started to boil in anger. Right away I told Desiderio about the incident and what the man had forced me to do. By coincidence my friend Desiderio knew this Negro very well and addressed him by his name: "Say, Crow, did you ever see this man before?" The Negro acted as if he had never seen me before and said so. But my friend Pérez insisted that he knew me. In addition, he said to him in English, "This is the man you ran off that cargo train last night about 10 this side of Sublin [Sublime] on the curve." "I don't know him," the Negro answered, "and, besides, the passenger train that he could have taken does not arrive until seven." "Nevertheless," repeated Pérez, "this is the man who begged you last night not to force him off the train and the one who told you he was not a hobo as you thought but a good man who was on his way to collect money the company owed him. But you would not listen and instead went out to get a pistol to kill him, according to what he told me. Then you threatened him by ordering him to jump, exposing him to be killed either that way or else by you. You could have let him ride and later reimburse you for the fare because he told you he would have money as soon as he got to Houston that same day." As Desiderio was talking to the Negro, I put my hand in my pocket and grabbed a fistful of gold coins and showed them to him. Desiderio continued saying, "He would gladly have paid you, and you would have gained a good new friend. Your action would have been approved by the good Lord," Pérez said, pointing toward the sky.

Dick, as the Anglos called Desiderio, knew that black people were very superstitious and the words he had been using would have some kind of effect, and so they did. The perverse Negro asked Pérez to please forgive him and to beg me to forgive him as well for his bad deed. He never intended to kill me but only to scare me and if he had understood that I was going to collect my pay, he would have let me stay on the train. Once again he asked for forgiveness for his mean action and more so after he found out I had arrived in Houston on a special train. Finally, after much begging for forgiveness for what he had done, we told him he was forgiven, provided he never did anything like that again. After that the Negro went on his way, and we went on ours.

Chapter 4

An *Opíparo* Breakfast

*An Incident Where Sometimes the Poor Can
Also Enjoy Magnificent Meals like the Rich*

W E WENT TO visit the family that I spoke of in the previous chapter. There [at their home] we met young Agustín, who invited us for a ride in a skiff on the bayou between Houston and Galveston. We accepted the invitation, rented the skiff, and boarded it. We went for about ten miles to where there was a very big camp of laborers who were clearing land with axes. This land was to be used for planting crops. When we were returning, a man of about thirty years of age joined us. He was carrying a small attractive blanket over his shoulder. He was dressed in an average manner, wearing pants made from French cashmere, which were very popular in those days, a good woolen shirt that would cost not less than three dollars, a good felt hat, small but well styled, and knee-high, worn-out, calf-leather boots underneath his pant legs.

When Dick and I saw him, he hailed us and asked how much we would charge to carry him back to Houston. The skiff owner said there was no charge but that he would accept his help with the oars. Immediately the man took hold of the oars and proved to be very skillful. Soon we arrived at Houston, and when we were ready to return the skiff, he was the first to ask how much the rental charge was, but we had paid the fee before we left the dock. After we landed, we all went to town. We went to drink a beer, and he insisted on paying for the entire expense, but we would not allow it. Afterward we went on an outing in the city, and around 10:30 P.M. Desiderio thought it was getting late and said it was about time to turn in. "We have had enough of an outing, and it's time to go to bed," he said. "As you wish," we all answered at the same time. By this time the unknown person we had just recently met had given us his name as Rodríguez. "If you wish, Mr. Rodríguez," I said, "to spend a bad night with us, come and join us at our lodging." "It wouldn't be any inconvenience to me as long as I am no bother to you all," he replied, "because I can always go to another place where I lodged before when I came to Houston." "But if you wish," Agustín said, "you can stay with me." "Thank you," answered Rodríguez, "I will accept young Gómez's invitation." So we ended our city walk and said farewell to Agustín, promising to meet him again at breakfast time. This would be at 7 in the morning at his home. Of course, we asked to be sure to have a delicious breakfast, which Rodríguez called "opíparo." Agustín, upon hearing that word, meekly told us that he did not know what that type of breakfast was.

Mr. Rodríguez, after being encouraged by a few beers he had consumed and still sitting around the table, stood up and asked permission to say a few words. "You may speak," answered Mr. Pérez solemnly. Then Rodríguez asked me to explain to Mr. Garza (that was Agustín's last name) what the word *opíparo* meant. That was an unexpected request, and for a moment I was dumbfounded, but suddenly, like a flash, I began to remember my language studies at school, and it came to mind that one of my schoolmates had at one time offered us an *opípara comida* [a magnificent dinner]. This was a reward to the best student who had the highest grades in the final examinations. It was a good thing I had kept a clear memory because it helped me out of that difficult situation. Without missing a beat, I immediately answered that the word *opíparo* signified "copious, splendid" and was used to describe dinner banquets given for dignified people who had been distinguished with high honors.

No sooner had I finished than Mr. Rodríguez extended his arm and said, "I congratulate you very cordially because you are quite correct" and patted my shoulder. But I assure you, dear readers, that I came out of that predicament by pure luck or, in other words, by accident. Dick, who was a critical rascal, laughed from ear to ear, and it seemed that he would not hush up.[1] Meanwhile, young Garza moved close to me and said, "It appears I will have to see that nothing is missing from this breakfast." "It is like this," I answered, "try to have a quart of good port wine—that must not be missing from the table. That should excite Mr. Rodríguez, who will be satisfied that such would be what he calls an 'opíparo almuerzo' [a magnificent breakfast]."

I put my hand into my pocket and brought out some gold coins and invited young Garza to take whatever was necessary to pay for the expense of the breakfast; he answered that it was not necessary because he would arrange for the meal himself. "That is okay," I replied, "but if you do not present an exact account of the expenses for the banquet, we will not be satisfied, nor will we accept the opíparo almuerzo."

In the meantime Mr. Rodríguez and Mr. Pérez had been observing us and thought we were discussing the breakfast expenses. They both approached us, ready to share the expenses, and asked us what the subject was. "If it is about money, we have some," they said. Agustín answered immediately that there was no need for anything, that everything was all right, and then thanked us. Finally we excused ourselves, and when we got to our lodgings, we asked the hotel manager to please bring another cot to the same room that my friend Pérez and I had rented. The room was quite big. There was room enough for four cots if need be.

Mr. Rodríguez was a worldly person. He had much experience in life, and we noted he was a smart man at making money because the way he would spend money gave his ability away. Finally Agustín left, having given his commitment to make us that opíparo almuerzo. The rest of the night we were awake since Mr. Rodríguez was a man of good judgment and enjoyed conversing with people he liked and spoke with such openness that it was clear he was speaking the truth. He spoke from the heart. He enjoyed a few drinks and had made sure to bring with him a quart of good whiskey—but it appeared we all had the same thought as each one of us had a small bottle of the same. But as far as I was concerned I always enjoyed the delicacy of a sip in the morning just at rising time right after I washed up to begin my day. That is to say, I enjoyed starting the morning right. Although my friend Pérez did not drink, he knew that I did, so he had also bought a small bottle. As you may well understand, we had enough drinks to last us until early morning.

VERY DELIGHTFUL CONVERSATIONS WITH FRIENDS

Where We Would Learn the Interesting Life of Rodríguez

We began a conversation that lasted from 11 that night in December 1890 until the following day at 6:30 in the morning. At this time we got dressed to go to the house of our good friend, Agustín Garza, who had gotten up at 5 in the morning to spruce up the kitchen and prepare the splendid banquet with the ingredients bought the night before. You may remember that I had made you aware of the celebrated quart of port wine. This had been a proper provision because Garza had not only prepared himself with port wine, he also had other kinds of liquors, gin, and cognac with of course the traditional *vino tinto* [red wine].

I believe that my curious readers would like to know what we talked about all night long on the eve of our celebrated breakfast. So then I will satisfy your wish by transferring to these pages textually what we talked about until daybreak. Pérez began talking some about places he had been working lately, but then Rodríguez asked if he had been employed by the Aransas Pass Company. My companion Pérez answered that he had worked for that company.

"I also worked for the company," said Rodríguez, "when it started operating in the Cuero, Texas, area. I left that job, and now I am on my way back to Cuero to visit a friend I have there."

"I am going back to Corpus Christi," answered Pérez, "and Gómez is going to Yoakum. Luckily we can all three be together for a few hours."

Since we had plenty of time, Desiderio started to share his life story with Rodríguez. He began by telling him where he was from and what he planned to do subsequently. Pérez continued talking and brought his conversation around to the moment we had met at the workers' camp on the edge of the bayou. It must have been 1:30 in the morning when Dick stopped talking, and then I started relating what had happened to me lately. Rodríguez then commented that he had seen me before when Tamez and I had worked on the construction of the bridge between Cuero and Goliad.

"Mr. Tamez is a skillful worker," said Rodríguez, "and he enjoys great fame around these parts of the country. You, Mr. Gómez, have a good partner in Tamez."

"Truly," I answered, "Tamez is a good companion, and that is why I preserve his friendship and will try to preserve it during the time before he goes to México, according to his wishes." At this moment I told him about the letter Tamez received from México and his anticipated marriage. Rodríguez showed great interest in the subject and praised the fidelity of Tamez's sweetheart. After taking a good swig, he proposed a toast to the good health of the future wife of my friend, Tamez, whose sweetheart was waiting for him with open arms to unite with the man who had promised to love her forever. Then we paused temporarily, which I excused because we had been drinking, and I asked Mr. Rodríguez, "What is happening, my friend Rodríguez? It appears you do not feel well."

"No, gentlemen," answered Rodríguez, "I feel perfectly well, but I find myself vividly impressed with what Gómez has said about the long wait of that woman for her absent love, a long wait that, according to my friend, has lasted more than five years. Truly this heroism must be underlined, and it is without a doubt a dignified action from a great woman. That is why at this moment I cannot do less than to pay tribute and profess my greatest admiration for this meritorious woman— Mr. Tamez's sweetheart." And while saying all this, he lifted up his bottle and drank a good swig of wine. "Whenever you see your friend Mr. Tamez," he continued, "congratulate him for me and tell him that sometime in the future I will have the opportunity to congratulate him in person."

Next I shared with him the story about the individual who stole from us more than four thousand dollars that belonged to more than fifty workmen and who then woke up the following morning in México trumpeting "La Golondrina" and how I had saved myself from that trap. He laughed heartily. Then I told him about the mysterious woman, and he said very thoughtfully, "Gómez, you are predestined to be a rich man because it can clearly be seen that God protects you."

A MULE LOADED WITH GOLD!

Rodríguez Finds a Treasure That He Had Need to Abandon

About three o'clock in the morning Rodríguez began to tell his story, which is truly interesting and verifiable. "I am from Tampico," Rodríguez began saying. "I was raised on the margins of the Pánuco River, where my first job was to operate the cargo transport canoes. When the elections of 1871 were held for the presidency of the Republic of México, there occurred disturbances that caused the call to arms of both parties who were not happy with the outcome of the elections between don Sebastián Lerdo de Tejada and don Porfirio Díaz. Luckily I had to become a soldier because there was a law that stated that all citizens had to serve five years as volunteers, and I joined the government forces that upheld the principles that were supportive of don Sebastián Lerdo de Tejada, who was the president. In a battle that took place near Palmillas in the state of Tamaulipas, the forces of don Porfirio beat the government forces, to which I belonged. During the confusion of battle, a comrade of mine and I decided to desert and took advantage of the first opportunity. When we saw the right time to desert, I told my comrade that now was the time to flee and to throw away our arms. Having done this, we started our desperate getaway toward the north—he in front and I behind. My friend must have been a fast runner because I could never catch up with him. Nonetheless, I ran and ran until I arrived at a small ravine where there was a fallen mule. I went closer to examine it and saw with great surprise that the cargo on top of the mule was all money, whose weight prevented that poor animal from getting back on its feet. When I began to examine it closely, I could see many little white canvas sacks full of pesos. The *rebujal* [a small vacant area between the harnesses] was full of *víboras* [long canvas sacks] that contained twenty-dollar gold coins. Then I took out my pocketknife, cut the ropes that tied the víboras to the harness, opened one of them—and was I shocked! They were full of gold coins! I soon pocketed a few coins and hung one of the víboras over my shoulder and ran to look for my friend, whom I never saw again, although they tell me he is still alive. I walked about two miles, and that money on my shoulder was getting heavy, immensely heavy. I never thought that money could be such a heavy load. But finally I decided to abandon it, so I did, throwing it into a deep precipice, and there that treasure is buried.

"Later I felt sorry and regretted it and became upset, thinking what would have become of me with the great treasure that God had probably put there in my way to enjoy. The nation had already lost it, but without a doubt another person less inept than I would soon meet up with that pile of gold. Furthermore, I should have noticed that poor miserable animal was surely going to die under that heavy load, and I could have saved it. And thinking back about the treasure, I think I could have buried it near where I had found it and come back and taken it out when things changed. But I did not do any of those things because I was thinking mostly at the time about saving myself, which I did, thank God, after my sad pilgrimage of more than eight days of grim suffering at its worst. Once in Texas, however, the first thing that came to mind was my stupidity at having abandoned the precious treasure that I did not enjoy. But now it was too late to think about it. The treasure had been lost!

"Finally I arrived for the first time at the great city of Brownsville. Without hesitation I entered a small restaurant and asked for something to eat for breakfast. Upon finishing my breakfast, I paid with one of those coins I had in my pocket. And, boy, was I surprised when they returned my change, which was nothing less than the fabulous amount of nineteen dollars and seventy-five cents [at that time the dollar and the peso were equal in value]. I felt an unknown feeling when I saw that amount of money, and I swear to you that I do not know what I felt because it was the most money I had ever had at one time in my whole life. When I put all that money in my pocket, all of the guests at the restaurant stared at me, attentively and surprised, and I could not tell whether they intended to kill me or just take away my fortune. I also thought that such awe would be what causes rich people to be admired when they show their money. The truth is, my friends, that at that moment I thought I was a millionaire and left the premises without giving a thank-you or saying a good-bye to anyone who was present. When I was out in the street, I noticed people were staring and some even laughing at me. After a while I found out why they were laughing at me and considered them justified because I was thoughtlessly talking to and answering myself—these were the effects caused by that great fortune! When I came to my senses, I went straight to the river's edge looking for an inconspicuous place to really turn loose of my excited thoughts. Then I entered a dense thicket and counted and counted my money many times. I added to the total five more coins I had in my pocket that Providence had urged me to take from the víbora that I later threw away into the precipice. Those coins in my possession amounted to more than one hundred pesos. Oh, what happiness! I went to the river's edge, washed my face, and drank some water in order to refresh myself. Afterward, my thoughts went back to the precious cargo on the mule that I had abandoned because of my uncommon cowardice and stupidity, so to speak. But I felt content to think there was no reason to feel desperate, as I was now free in the state of Texas and with more than a hundred bucks in my pocket. I really considered myself truly rich, and I was not asking favors of anyone."

It was four o'clock in the morning when Mr. Rodríguez ended his story. Dick went to sleep immediately, but as much as we tried to imitate him, we could not fall asleep. We did not know why, but we thought it was because of the effects of the whiskey. When we realized we could not sleep, we kept on talking in low voices so as not to disturb Pérez and his sweet dreams, and Rodríguez continued relating his story more or less as a secret until he arrived in Central Texas, ending his narration at the moment we met him at the edge of the small stream that ties Houston with Galveston. At the end of his tale he said to me, "You see, Gómez, how I was predestinated to be a poor man for the rest of my life. How correct the old adage is that says, 'good fortune knocks on your door only once.' He who knows how to take advantage of it may be forever happy, and he who lets it pass him by will live in adversity as long as he exists. I am sure that I am one of those that allow good fortune to pass by, and I accept my fate. That is why I urge myself to measure the planet through the continent without a sure sign indicating the end of my journey."

Truthfully, I share with you, dear readers, the fact that Mr. Rodríguez's story left me very impressed, in particular his last words relative to his future. Mr. Rodríguez had a powerful reason to feel sad about his bad luck, which we will find out later on.

At 6 in the morning we began to clean up and comb our hair. Afterward we got dressed but being careful to be as quiet as possible so as not to awaken Desiderio. Dick was a wily old fox that never slept late, for his life belonged to a hard worker who was well liked by people of high esteem. We could do nothing else but immerse ourselves in these straightforward manners and respect him for his unflagging honesty. No sooner had we started to move than he sat up in his bed; at this time Mr. Rodríguez was washing up out in the corridor. The first thing Pérez wanted to know was what had happened to the mule that had been loaded with treasure—it was at that point that he had fallen asleep. Pérez began to laugh heartily, which was characteristic of him. When he stopped laughing, Rodríguez asked him, "What would you have done with that gold-laden mule?" "I would have relieved that poor animal of the heavy load that was squashing it," answered Pérez. In addition, after a long pause Rodríguez asked Pérez, "What else would you have done?" "Oh, nothing more," answered Dick, and he added, "About taking the money, I would have been too scared to take anything!" "Well, that is what happened to me," said Rodríguez immediately, and we all laughed. Then Dick, while still in bed, reached under the cot, took out a pint of good whisky that had not yet been opened, and said when he found out we had not had a wink of sleep all night, "Now all of you are going to drink to my health and to honor all the best night-watchers of Houston!" We all had a good swallow of that whiskey and then hurried to get dressed to be on time at the Garza residence, where the magnificent breakfast awaited us, as had been announced by Mr. Rodríguez.

At 6:30 we left the premises and went in the direction of the

Garza family's house, about six blocks from where we were. The Garza family was composed of four members: don Agustín, the patriarch of the family that carried his name; his wife, doña Soledad Mireles de Garza; a young lady, Evangelina, about seventeen years old; and the young man, Agustín. Today Rodríguez's famous opíparo breakfast would be celebrated.

When we arrived, we were graciously welcomed and invited in with much friendliness. We had not had the pleasure of meeting the young lady the previous afternoon as she was employed at a milliner's and her workday ended at 6 in the afternoon. That is why we had unfortunately not seen her the day before. She would start her workday at 8:30 every morning, so we would have the pleasure of her company at breakfast time. Pérez had already told me that Evangelina was a beautiful and amiable creature. She was an enchanting being and well educated. She had a limited understanding of English but a good command of the Spanish language because her mother was a teacher and don Agustín had been a distinguished person in Mexican politics. When Mr. Sebastián Lerdo de Tejada became a refugee in the United States, don Agustín also had to immigrate to the United States, but he had high hopes of soon returning to his country.

After all the presentations of the guests were made, they invited us to the table, which had already been set by Evangelina's neat, beautiful hands, and the food, whose appetizing aroma was filling the air, had been prepared by doña Soledad, who was an expert in the culinary arts. Then we all took our respective chairs, opened the bottle of port wine, served full glasses of wine to each of the participants, and began with the toasts. Rodríguez was the first to offer a toast to the well-being of the Garza-Pérez family and to the good health of the beautiful Evangelina; I followed with a toast to the good health and unequaled beauty of Evangelina, who flushed upon hearing my words. Mr. Garza happily applauded, which was followed by general merriment. Doña Soledad was visibly moved because, at that moment, she was thinking of her beloved México and commented that, as things were happening, she felt she would never see her beloved land again! She was a native of Victoria, Tamaulipas, México, and was a close relative of General don Rómulo Cuéllar, who was the governor of that state. Mr. Rodríguez was very happy, but we did not know why; was it because we all were thinking of México, or was it was the effect of the cognac? You see, the second bottle was already more than half empty. Next we began savoring that delicious and magnificent breakfast with hearty appetites.

The good humor gradually increased, and the family was extremely happy, with Mrs. Garza saying that her whole family was sincerely grateful that we were honoring them with our visit. She said that this was the happiest day she had had while living in Texas because she was surrounded by patriots sitting at her table who were enjoying a sincere and pleasant conversation. All of this was the reason for her immense happiness.

When we concluded our breakfast, we thanked them, but before we got up, I asked young Garza if he had the list of expenses for the breakfast. He then took out of his shirt pocket a paper on which the total amount was listed; it was as follows: 5 pounds of round steak, 75¢; three dozen eggs, 75¢; 2 pounds of bacon, 50¢; 2 heads of lettuce, 16¢; 2 pounds of tomatoes, 20¢; 1 jar of mayonnaise, 15¢; 1 jar of mustard, 15¢; 5 pounds of potatoes, 15¢; 1 pound of onions, 5¢; 3 pounds of cheese, 60¢; 1 prepared chicken, 85¢; 2 quarts of milk, 20¢; 1 pound of pea berry coffee, 20¢; 1 quart of port wine, $2.00; 1 bottle of gin, $1.50; 1 bottle of cognac, $1.50; ice, 10¢; sugar, 25¢; and preparation of the breakfast, $1.50. The total came to $11.56.

When I finished reading the list, I said out loud, "$11.56." Mr. Rodríguez quickly took out his wallet and said that the entire expense was his alone. "It was I who proposed the breakfast," he said, "and I baptized it with the name 'opíparo,' a word that Mr. Gómez explained correctly."

Doña Soledad, who knew nothing of our previous understanding, said she believed everything was already taken care of and there was no need for restitution of any kind. Pérez, who had also collected more than five hundred dollars from the company for two years of work, took out his wallet and said that money was not to be the cause of any difficulty. He laid his bag full of gold coins in the center of the table because indeed we had been paid in coins that shone more brightly than the sun itself.

"Gentlemen," said Rodríguez, "I will take care of the breakfast expenses, and I will *bialo solo* [dance alone]!" meaning that he and he alone would take care of the cost. I know very well that Rodríguez was *todo un hombre* [all man], that he deserved that honored appellation, and I understood there was nothing more to discuss. I was not mistaken because Rodríguez's requested action was followed by dropping on the table a twenty-peso gold coin. I then asked permission to speak, took a pencil, and wrote the following verse, which I beg my readers to excuse because it was passionately improvised while I was under the influence of the warmth of those sweet friends. Three stanzas were dedicated to Miss Garza because she was the soul of the family and the fiesta:

Décima
Dedicated to the beautiful Evangelina Garza
You are the beacon that illuminates your home,
Whom we, your happy guests,
Closely, we have come to honor;
Humbly asking, do not feel offended,
As today is the beginning, out of friendship, of a sphere
Which rapidly crosses the Universe,
Naming you with pleasures, the treasurer
Of the sum that was spent on this breakfast . . .
Congratulations and patience on your profession
And may everything progress successfully![2]

Don Agustín took the written poem and, having read it, Mr. Rodríguez exclaimed in a high voice, "I accept Gómez's proposal that Evangelina be the treasurer." Dick also spoke, saying that this small gift would grow if continual savings were added, which would provide earnings in the future. He added that he wanted to be one of the contributors to that savings box and added a five-peso coin to the twenty-peso coin already in the center of the table. At that moment Mr. Garza got up and read the décima, which was graciously received by everyone present. Then he addressed his daughter as follows: "Señorita Evangelina Garza, dearly appointed treasurer, you are now unconditionally responsible for the savings box that has been arranged with the contributions offered by these disinterested persons who have greatly honored our home with their courteous visit, for which we are eternally grateful because these gentlemen are interested only in the aggrandizement of their *raza* [race, people]." Doña Soledad also made use of the spoken word to thank us and to assure us that the treasure hereby acquired had been left in good hands and that it would multiply without fail.

After breakfast we all got up to prepare to leave, but before we did, I also took out from my pocket a five-peso gold coin and added it to the newly born savings box. Pérez had set the example, and I wanted to imitate him. We then excused ourselves from the Garza family with the promise that we would soon return. As we were leaving, Miss Garza said, "But you will return, right, Mr. Gómez?" As she was saying those words, she cast at me one of those looks that can kill a person but without out a pistol!

It was about eight in the morning when we left the home of the Garza family. The train that was to take us to our destination would leave about 8:40, which gave us enough time, but without hesitation we went to the railroad station, where we encountered many people. As soon as we arrived, two gentlemen approached us and asked us if we were workingmen, and I responded affirmatively. Rodríguez and Pérez kept on walking ahead and found a bench and sat down. One of the Americans, the older one, said to me, "I am looking for a good man who wants to be contracted to cut about 500 or 1,000 cords of wood that I need. I have some land from which all that wood needs to be removed. The land is no less than sixty acres, with some acres that may produce as many as 15 cords of wood."

"And how much do you pay per cord?" I asked him.

"Come on over and sit and let us talk," he answered. Then we went to sit on one of those benches at the center of the park, and he added: "I cannot tell exactly how many cords of wood we can get out of the brush, but whatever amount is taken out, I will offer you $1.25 for each cord." I liked the price. Then I told him I was a contractor and that our camp was not close by and that my companion and I were actually about to finish a fence-building contract but that as soon as we did so, we would accept his contract if we could come to an agreement. "I am sure we can agree," he answered. "It all depends on your seeing the land. If you wish, we can take the next train that comes by at 10, which goes down to my town of Flatonia. I will pay your fare to there. You see, it encourages me that you see the work that I am offering. After that, you can take the train that comes from Waco on the way to San Antonio, and you can be in Yoakum this very day." "Very well," I said, "but let me talk to my waiting companions as they are going to board the next train, and I will return right away."

As soon as I approached Rodríguez and Pérez, I said to them, "There has been a program change." "Why?" both asked at the same time. "Because I am not going with you on the same train," I answered. "I am now going to Flatonia with an American who has offered me a good job." "Do not waste time. Buy your tickets, and soon we will have an opportunity to write to each other." Immediately we all got our little writing pads out, and we each wrote our respective addresses so we could write to each other. We then said an emotional good-bye because at this time the conductor was already signaling the engineers to start the train. Again we said farewell with a simple "hasta la vista" for the second time.

Mr. Goethre (the name of the American) invited me to go downtown with him since we had ample time to do so because it was only 8:40 and our train was not due until 10. Therefore, we had enough time. We returned to the railroad station before the train arrived. It came on time, and we immediately embarked, reaching Flatonia at 2 in the afternoon. A carriage belonging to Mr. Goethre was already waiting for us. A Negro was the coachman, and he took us about five miles out of town to where the work to be done was located. After I looked over the terrain, we arranged everything in a few words, and I agreed to stay and to commence working immediately. Circumstances were favorable, as there were enough workingmen in the area to whom I had already talked when we arrived in Flatonia. The workers were ready to start laboring the following day if I so desired. They themselves encouraged me to accept the contract because there were plenty of *brazos* [arms] available. They were ready and had their necessary axes. Many of them had camping equipment, so many of their families could accompany them also.

After everything was arranged with the American, I wrote my friend Tamez and made him aware of things. I suggested that he finish the fence-building contracts as soon as possible and join me. He immediately answered me, saying he had already finished his contract and that all he needed to wrap up was to make two extra gates the company had requested. He had assigned four men to make the gates and had ordered the rest of the personnel to break camp. He had already requested a hauling wagon to begin loading—and that if luck was favorable, he would be with me the following day, God willing. Tamez would bring a company of twenty men and some of their families, provisions, beds, a kitchen, and many kinds of tools.

There was a distance of fifty miles between Yoakum and Flatonia on the road to Waco. Everything came out as my friend had said: The whole camp arrived on the 5 P.M. freight train at Flatonia. I already had the *wagins* [wagons] ready that would carry us to the workplace that very night.

NOTES

1. Translator's note: In the Spanish text, Gómez refers to Dick as a "criticón de siete suelas" [a critic of seven soles, or out-and-out rascal] and "a dos carrillos" [from cheek to cheek], thus leading me to translate the sentence as I have.

2. A *décima* [ten] is a poem of ten lines.

Chapter 5

The Company "Tamez-Gómez, Contractors" Signs Very Lucrative New Contracts

A S SOON AS our people arrived at the new camp, they began work cutting wood. I had already begun the project with ten men who were added to the twenty that Tamez had brought along, giving us a total of thirty men who made nine hundred cords of wood within fifteen days for a total of $1,125 at $1.25 per cord. We paid the working people $675, leaving us with a profit of $450 for fifteen days of work. A beautiful return, right? Then we made preparations for my companion to travel to México, where his promised one was waiting. He had already notified them to expect him.

We were paying our workers when two agents seeking contractors for two different projects arrived. One was a "rock" contract where ten* *gondolas* [freight cars] were needed to transport the materials that were to be used in the Port of Galveston, which was under construction. They would pay $50 for each carload. The other project was to prepare "life-OK" posts that were to be removed with steel drills and dynamite.[1] These two projects came from Mr. Goethre's kindness, the owner of the cordwood job who had recommended the "Tamez-Gómez contractors" to them. He told the agents that this company had cut nine hundred cords of wood within fifteen days and that he

---

*Note [in the original text]: This page includes an error that says that there were ten gondolas, but it should say one hundred gondolas. Let this be on record.

was very satisfied with the outcome of the project and that he would recommend them with much pleasure.

"We implore you gentlemen," we said to the two agents who had offered us the two projects, "to give us some time to work on a proposal to the rock project agent."

"I don't have much time to lose," said the rock project agent. "It is urgent that I notify the company regarding what I have done on this matter by 10 tomorrow morning and to board the train that same night to Galveston. However, I believe it behooves you to take this job because this is the place where the rock is located. Furthermore, you already have your workers well organized, therefore, with good luck, I will expect your answer by tomorrow morning at 10."

The other agent was a young businessman from Flatonia who was employed by a friend who owned the "life-OK" posts. This latter one lived in another county, but, knowing we had already finished the cordwood project, the first one entrusted him with the responsibility of finding some workers for him. The owner of the life-OK posts had told the young man to let us know about his *postas* project while taking advantage of the opportunity that the rock project agent was also coming to see us about. After a few doubtful moments we said to the rock project agent, "Then wait for us until tomorrow to give you both an answer."

"Very well," said the posts agent. "This way you can discuss the lumber issue with my boss," and having said that, both agents returned to the city.

After we finished paying all our workmen, we went to our tents to further discuss our personal affairs. We had already agreed that my companion Tamez would make his trip to the Republic of México, where his sweetheart was waiting so they could unite their destiny forever. My friend's sweetheart was named Espectación García, a very patient and faithful lady who had been waiting for the return of her loved one for more than five years.

The two new projects that came about made us gradually change our much-considered and well-developed plans. We started working on the proposals for the rock project that my companion Tamez liked so much since he had been a rock crusher back in his homeland, where he had had more than fifty employees in his charge.

Here is what we agreed upon: If they would allow us six weeks, we would accept the project. However, the company was offering $5,000 for one hundred train carloads of rock, which had to be completed within four weeks or about thirty days. This was an urgent project. The rock was needed badly; this is why they were offering so much. We talked to the employees we already had. There were about a hundred men, but not all of them were interested in working rock. Mr. Tamez finally offered $2.50 for a ten-hour workday. The company would furnish the rock and would set the rails where the workers would prepare the rock to be loaded. Some of those rocks were so big that four of them would fill up a single train-car.

After discussing the subject for a while, we went to bed already resolved that we would accept the contract. It was to be one hundred train carloads of rock for $5,000 and our commitment to complete the project within thirty days. We decided to pay the personnel on a daily basis instead of the thirty-day-schedule practice. The following day we went to town to see the rock project agent. We signed the contract and were told that a gentleman from town would show us where to start working. In the meantime the workers would arrive so we would have the supplies ready to load.

An Unexpected Meeting with Mr. Stafford

The Mysterious Petite Woman Appears on the Scene Again

When I went to speak to the businessman who had the posts project, I was told he was in town and that he would soon appear there. "But, of course," he further commented, "I already told him that you would be here today at 10, and there are still fifteen minutes to go." I waited a few moments, and then suddenly, to my great surprise, I met face to face with Mr. Stafford. This was the same American who, three weeks ago, had taken me like we were flying to catch up with the special train. That is, before my eyes was the husband of the mysterious petite lady who had persuaded him to make sure that I got to Houston on time to get paid by the company. As soon as he saw me, he said,

"Oh, we are old friends, and it so happens I have a request that my wife wanted me to make if I happened to see you, and that is, my wife wants to speak more leisurely with you." "She may be right," I answered, "because I did not return even to thank her." "Oh no, sir, that is not the reason," he answered, "she merely wants to know more about you." "Well," I answered, "I will speak to my partner, and I believe I will be there soon." As I said this, I went to talk to my friend and explained to him what was happening.

It so happened that not all of our workmen wanted to do rock work. Knowing the posts project was available, many preferred to work on this latter job, so under these circumstances we decided to accept both projects, and I would meet my commitment with the necessary workmen on the posts project. The rest of the workers, which was the larger group, would work on the rock project since they liked the $2.50 per day being offered. I would continue keeping the books for both units even if I had to travel every Monday on the morning Eagle Lake train, a trip of only forty miles, and return early that evening after spending most of the day at the rock project.

After all of this was clearly understood, I told Mr. Stafford I would take the posts job if I could move my company group that same day, and when the job was finished I would get all of my workmen ready at the station to be transported elsewhere. Mr. Stafford accepted everything I proposed and promised to send me a wagon pulled by two mule teams and two black men to help us move. "Today is Wednesday," he said to me. "Wait for the car on Friday, and we can move you between Saturday and Sunday so you can hopefully start your project on Monday." After we had finished our conversation, we parted, and my associate Tamez and I immediately went back to the camp to be with Mr. Worker, the name of the person responsible for the rock source and the man who was going to show us where to begin the operation.

The next day all of our people began getting ready. We had to go to town right away to arrange with the grocery store to send a clerk to camp to take the necessary orders for items we needed since we had to work all day Saturday. When we returned to camp, Mr. Tamez, my partner, said, "Do me a favor, and write my father and tell him to forgive me, but I will not be able to arrive as promised because an unexpected commitment has appeared that prevents me from keeping my word with him, but that I believe this is going to be much better for me and my promised one as I will have more resources to pay for our marriage expenses. Also, please ask my fiancée's family to forgive me and to be patient with me and tell them I will be with them within five or six weeks, God willing."

I wrote the letter as my friend wished, and then we went to town again to mail it and to talk to several of our workers who lived there. We wanted to tell them they could start the following morning at 7 and stop at 6 with one hour at noon for lunch and rest and that each one would earn $2.50 every day. This rock project was well known, for it was well paid, and the people were very excited because in those days the daily wages were $1.25 per day. But Mr. Tamez was satisfied with a small profit so as to complete the project as soon as possible and have enough funds to go to his promised one and to "get out of being poor," as he would often say.

The novelty of the rock project created great interest among the Fayette County population. Many came seeking employment. There was no shortage of workers for Mr. Tamez, who fortunately finished the project in twenty-eight days after completing the one hundred train carloads of rock that were needed to finish the Galveston wharf. The wages for the workmen and other expenses amounted to $4,525. He received payment of $5,000, giving him a net profit of $475. This was accomplished within twenty-eight work days with one hundred workers, with many leaving the job before it was completed; some left because it was a hard and heavy job, and others quit because they did not like it. Nevertheless, the ones that left were not actually missed because the job did not require them. By the last week of the project, only thirty workmen remained.

As I mentioned before, while talking with Mr. Stafford, he promised to send the wagon and the black men to move us out on Friday. I waited for him that day, but we were moved the following Sunday morning. We arrived at our designated place without any problems, and with God's permission we prepared to start work on Monday. I started working with ten men that came along with me. We were making 250 posts a day, and we completed our project more or less at the same time Tamez finished his rock project, but I also made a contract to build a new three-mile-long fence.

At last we made arrangements for my associate's trip to México, and on February 14, 1891, he left for China, Nuevo León, with the intent of marrying the honorable Miss Espectación García. Meanwhile I continued with my fence-building project. But before continuing, I must share with you the question, what was Mrs. Stafford's curiosity in wanting to talk to me? This lady wanted to see me, but I did not know in what manner I could be of service to her given my humble status, which it truly was, compared to the social sphere to which she belonged. As I said before, we arrived on Sunday morning at Mr. Stafford's farm, and right away we were shown the rooms the workmen and their families were going to occupy. My living quarters were going to be in the main house. After they showed them to me, I was invited to eat with them at noon.

After sitting around the table, Mrs. Stafford told me she was curious about my background. She believed that I was not a common man and undoubtedly had an interesting story, which she wanted to hear even if it took a long time. That is to say, she wanted me to share my life story with her from the time I was born until I arrived at her place. She wanted me to tell her where I was born, who my parents were, if they still lived, where was I educated, whether I was a religious person, and what denomination I belonged to. She was saying all this in the presence of her husband. She added that if it was not inconvenient for me to satisfy her curiosity, she in turn was willing to share her story from the time she was a small child until the moment I arrived at her home that morning, which held gratifying memories for me.

Her husband, who I had never heard talk with such interest, laughed and said that even he was interested in knowing her life story from her own lips, which would be very interesting to hear. "It is so," she commented, "and I would be very happy if you would honor us with your attention, for I am sure you would be pleased. But in the meantime, I invite you to first listen to Mr. Gómez's own life story." "Yes," said Mr. Stafford, "but first I want him to tell us about his Houston trip." "Very well," I answered. "The special train you put me on arrived in Houston at 1:15, and before 2 that afternoon I had all my money in my pocket. For this I am very grateful to you for your goodness, after I reimburse you for whatever expense you incurred." "To her," said Mr. Stafford, motioning toward his wife. "No, sir, you do not owe me anything for what I did for you," replied Mrs. Stafford, "and I am deeply happy that you received all the money coming to you." "Thank you," I answered, "I am much indebted for your services, and I wish with all my heart to pay for the great assistance you provided me. If in any dignified manner I can repay you, please let me know, and I will be at you disposal to help you in whatever manner you wish."

After saying this, I proceeded to tell them what had happened to me with the Negro brakeman who denied that he was the one who had thrown me from the train as we rounded that railroad curve. I told them how he claimed he could not have been the same man because the passenger train had yet to arrive in Houston and that not even a freight train had arrived since he had taken up his position on the train. The Staffords laughed heartily when I told them that, after arguing with him for a while, Pérez told him that God would repay him for his bad conduct and that he had done wrong in throwing me off that train. These words affected him tremendously, and he trembled even more when he found out I had arrived on the special train at one o'clock. Without a doubt he figured I must be a very influential person and that the special train had picked me up, while he himself had ignored the arrival of that train.

When I finished telling them that incident, the couple shared looks and laughed. I further added that the Negro had asked for my forgiveness several times as he seemed to be very upset. When I finished relating these last details, I repeated my apologies for not having returned to thank them for rendering their wonderful services and told them about the wood contract, which had led me to travel via another line.

After eating our dinner and before getting up from the table, we agreed to tell our respective life stories the following Monday, at night, from 7 to 9, and that I should be the first one to begin. We excused ourselves, and I went to my lodgings.

The following day, as I said before, we started the posts project, which I completed at about the same time my friend Tamez finished with his rock contract. We had to go a mile to where our posts-cutting job was, but we were riding a wagon with all the necessary equipment and water supplies. At noon we would return to eat, and at 1:30 we would go back to our project and return from work just before dark.

At last the day and hour arrived when we were to share our stories. At 7 P.M., I began to tell my humble history in the following terms: "I was a legitimate son of Simón Gómez and Juanita Acosta, both originally from Linares, Nuevo León, México. I was born on June 21, 1865, at a hacienda in the state of Tamaulipas named La Gavia, which was the property of Fructuoso Susaya, a Spaniard. I was baptized there at the same hacienda. When I was a young child, my parents brought me to the heroic city of Matamoros, Tamaulipas. I was raised in Matamoros until the age of eighteen, when I decided to venture out after studying at the San Juan Elementary School, where I received my primary instruction. My father had participated in the political arena, and as a result we ended up very poor. This situation encouraged me to go out and seek my fortune to be of some help to my parents, and I left with my parents' blessing on June 14, 1884. That same day I crossed the Rio Bravo in order to enter the state of Texas."

At this point in my story, Mrs. Stafford asked, "What important change occurred in the national administration that year?" Right away I knew the Staffords were well versed regarding events in the politics of my country, and I answered, "Don Manuel González was going to again relinquish his government to General Porfirio Díaz. After all, he was coming to the end of his presidential term, having been in power since the year of 1880." "Don Manuel González, *el manco* [a one-armed person]," Mrs. Stafford said with interest, "because they say he was missing an arm." "Exactly, ma'am, he is missing an arm," I answered. Then Mrs. Stafford asked again, "What other noted act took place during his administration?" "Well, it was the establishment of the *moneda de níquel* [nickel money], something that the people became profoundly disgusted with, after which they protested en masse in front of the national palace to demand its elimination. President González then appeared at the center of the multitude and with much courage and great valor stood in front of the insurgents and promised he would remove from circulation the money the people did not want." "Exactly," said Mrs. Stafford, "and now don Porfirio will obtain the presidency for the second time and will remain in power until he enthrones himself, which appears to be his intention."

(Mrs. Stafford was right in thinking that way, for we all know that don Porfirio received a second term when don Manuel González turned over the power to him. Don Porfirio then established a dictatorship, remaining in that position until 1911, when the revolution captained by don Francisco I. Madero forced him to relinquish it. Then don Porfirio left México for Paris, France, where he later died in 1915.)

"I met the wife of don Porfirio," Mrs. Stafford continued saying, "when she was on her way to New Orleans on a vacation. She stopped at Victoria, Texas, and visited the mother superior of the convent, who was a very close friend of hers since she held the same position in a convent in León, Guanajuato, México. Mrs. Díaz is a very kind person and extremely amiable."

When Mrs. Stafford said these last words, my admiration for her increased immeasurably because it was obvious she was well versed in the current political happenings of my country; she referred to other Mexican historical events I had not believed a foreigner who lived away from the hustle and bustle of the big cities would be aware of. Of course, the questions she asked me in reference to the government of General Manuel González made me feel uneasy when trying to answer them because they were presented unexpectedly, but since I was familiar with those events, I was able to successfully ease my way out of that predicament with honor.

"But please forgive me for interrupting you," Mrs. Stafford said suddenly, "and, I beg you, please continue with your story, which is very interesting to me." "With great pleasure, ma'am," I answered. "Once in Brownsville, which was one of the largest cities within the margins of the Rio Grande, I tried to continue my expedition. I looked for a way to find someone who was on his way to Central Texas. I knew that wagons or people on horseback frequently traveled north. I then heard that a carriage was going to Victoria, Texas, commissioned to bring some students back to their homes in Brownsville. I talked to the coachman and informed him that I needed to travel to the center of Texas to find employment. Since he was going in that direction, I told him that I would appreciate it if he would take me, that I could help as his assistant, and that I was familiar with handling and harnessing beasts of burden. The coachman answered me peevishly that he did not need anyone. I thanked him and walked away.

"The following day I asked for directions to Corpus Christi, and having well understood the travel information, I started to walk with confidence and high hopes. Soon after, now on the road, I noted the fresh tracks of a carriage that was ahead of me, and I thought maybe this was the man who was on his way to Victoria to bring back the students and who had refused to take me. I walked all day, and just before sunset I arrived at a ranch called El Peñascal. There I asked permission to spend the night. Luckily I met some good people, and they did not deny me hospitality. I spent the night at this ranch, and, after getting up the next morning, I gave haircuts to the men of the house. These included the father-in-law and son-in-law. These men had found out the night before that I was a barber since the only luggage I had was a bundle where I carried scissors, combs, and a brush. After finishing my job, they invited me for breakfast, and later they prepared me a good lunch for the road, which consisted of meat and tortillas.

"I got back on the road and did not stop until noontime. I sat down under some shade trees, and there I rested for a while. As I was getting ready to continue on my way, I saw a wagon pulled by four mules coming my way, loaded with cedar posts. I waited at the edge of the road, and when it was in front of me, the coachman greeted me and asked me where I was going. I answered that I was going further ahead and that I was searching for a job. 'If you like,' he said, 'I will take you where you can find employment, that is, if you know how to work.' I answered that I had never worked for anyone else besides my father and brothers at home. He then asked me where I was from and how old I was. I answered all of his questions while we were under way and I was sitting on the posts, while he was riding on his saddled mule.

Brownsville riverfront, 1863, as seen from the Mexican side, showing a ferry that during the nineteenth century brought people and goods to what Luis Gómez described as "one of the largest cities within the margins of the Rio Grande." From *Frank Leslie's Illustrated Famous Leaders and Battle Scenes of the Civil War* (New York: Mrs. F. Leslie, 1896), 412.

"At dark we arrived at an encampment where about fifty men were employed making fences that a Corpus Christi company was building and that went all the way to the sea. 'I believe you can find employment here,' said the coachman. 'At least you can continue your trip up north from this place with more ease because every day people leave from here on their way to the north. The manager of this camp sometimes looks for someone to help him make wage payments, and that day is very near.' When we arrived at the camp that night, he recommended me to several of his friends, including Mr. Tamez, whom I saw here for the first time."

Here at this point I told the Staffords the story of Mr. Tamez, who is already well known to my readers. As I was relating this tale to my protectors, I imagined that my companion Tamez was already enjoying his honeymoon. At this point in my story, Mrs. Stafford asked me what my religious beliefs were. "I am Catholic," I answered. "I follow the same religious beliefs as my parents, but I must confess I do not sympathize with the clergy." The Staffords laughed at hearing my last few words, at which time the lady exclaimed, "I see, but let us continue. You were saying at the beginning of your story that you had come to this country with the intention of working to help your parents back home as soon as you could find employment. Did you do it?" "Yes, ma'am," I answered. "On July 4, 1884, I mailed the first registered letter with a $5 money order to my father in H. Matamoros, México, which was received without misfortune. My father replied immediately, which was of great joy to me. The second remittance was made from Cuero, Texas, for an $11 money order in the month of September of the same year, and that was done continuously, without my ever forgetting them. On December 24, 1887, I went to visit them personally and took them money and clothing and many other things, for I was already working for the Aransas Pass Company by this time. I did so while we were building a railroad branch from Skidmore to Alice, taking advantage of the proximity to go see my parents.

"I returned to my job, and immediately after that the company moved to the other side of the Brazos River to a small town named Fulchers [Fulshers], Fort Bend County. That was where we were robbed by that old friend that arrived in México at daybreak the following morning while singing 'La Golondrina.' (My listeners thoroughly enjoyed this anecdote about the thief.) From there we finished and left for Yoakum early in the morning and stayed there until the company sold its interests to another one, announcing that it would pay everything that was owed to the workers. The rest of my story you already know."

"Thank you," said the two spouses, and Mrs. Stafford said, "Tomorrow I will share with you my own story, and I am sure you are going to enjoy it." As she said this, she looked at her husband, knowing quite well that he would be interested in hearing the story about her childhood and afterward. Although she had already shared most of it with him, I was sure he would take pleasure in hearing it more in detail.

NOTE

1. "Life-OK" was probably a mispronunciation of "live oak," although live oak wood seems to have rarely been used for posts. Since this mispronunciation is likely, the reference to using "steel drills and dynamite" may well indicate confusion by either Gómez or the printer with the tools needed for the rock project.

Chapter 6

The Phantom!

A Comical Historical Incident That Sounds Like a Tall Tale

A S SOON AS Mrs. Stafford mentioned that she would begin to share her history the following day, I interrupted her by saying, "If you wish to stay awake for a while, I will share with you an interesting anecdote, and although it is a true story, it may sound like a tall tale. I am sure you are going to have a good laugh."

"Yes, sir," said Mrs. Stafford. "Tell us that anecdote, and we will listen with much pleasure." Her husband also said, while getting comfortable in his chair, "Bring on that story!"

"Well, then, here I go," I said and began in this manner: "When I was barely a ten-year-old child, my father wanted me to learn some useful things. He had a good friend who was a traveling salesman; that is, he went to farm after farm selling or exchanging his merchandise for hides, eggs, cheese, chickens, jerky, and even hog bristles and wool. His name was Eleuterio Garza, and he and my father agreed that I would accompany don Eleuterio on his frequent trips throughout the rural community.

"Mr. Garza was well known throughout the area because he was a just and friendly man. He had been a municipal official in his hometown for many years, and when he left his employment, he left like all just men: poor. He was called *Filántropo* as a nickname in the city, and perhaps because of his generosity he ended up very poor. Anyway, don Eleuterio was forced to become a traveling salesman. He used a small cart of the kind called *rabones* [short tailed]. It was pulled by a male mule that, although it was somewhat old, could pull its load with ease. The cart was loaded with groceries, clothing, shoes, hats, quilts, and a few medicines. We had already made a few trips, and Mr. Eleuterio was well pleased with my services, and so were my parents because he would always tell them that I was a very intelligent boy and that I would become a great businessman some day.

"And that is how things were going until, one afternoon at sunset, we arrived at a big ranch where we usually stopped regardless of the time of the day. Mr. Garza would always spend the night there, and sometimes we would stay there for as many as three days because he had a large clientele to serve in this place. As I have already said, we arrived as it was getting dark, and before the old mule finished gobbling its fodder, it was completely dark. I had to take the animal to pasture near a lake about five hundred yards away from where we were staying. The way to get to the lake was down a very narrow trail. This was the only way to get there because the cacti and the woods were very dense in some places. When the animal finished eating, a young boy about my age and who was a good friend of mine helped me pasture the mule. After playing for a while, we leisurely returned to the place we were staying, and my friend was taking the lead and telling me about a rabid coyote that had escaped along this same trail after biting all of the dogs at the ranch. This had happened about a week ago. I then told him that the cactus thicket was very dense, and if the coyote felt like returning to this area, we did not have a way to escape. 'But that coyote is not coming back,' I said, 'because I heard they killed it at the neighboring ranch of San Antonio.'

"That is as far as that conversation went because he suddenly stopped and said, 'Good Lord! What is that I see down the trail? The phantom!' he exclaimed, and without hesitation he jumped into the cactus patch to his left, and I followed him. That poor soul was opening a new trail through the dense wall of cactus and *tasajillo*.[1] Only a person possessed by desperation and fear would do such a foolish thing. I followed my buddy in his frantic escape, and I got to see the phantom that had terrified him. Truly it was fearsome because I was able to see a dark body with a bright white face similar to alabaster with reflections that reached the sky and touched the stars, leaving no doubt in my mind that my friend had a very good reason to be frightened.

"When I got back to camp, Mr. Garza was pulling the bed from the cart, and I told him what had happened. 'I believe,' I said, 'that boy is badly mangled because in his escape he had no respect for the cactus or the tasajillo.' The boy's mother, who had just gotten to where we were but was not seen by us, overheard me when I told the incident to Mr. Eleuterio. At that moment the boy also appeared. 'Dear holy mother!' said the mother when she saw him. 'What happened to you, son of my life?' as she started crying along with her son. Alarmed at the sound of the screams, the neighbors began pouring out of their homes fully armed with rifles. The boy was laid on a quilt on the ground, and the grandmother started removing all of the thorns by the light of the lamps some of the neighbors had brought. I also felt a lot of thorns on my clothing and was very uncomfortable. Everybody was asking me what I had seen, while I answered that the boy had said it was a phantom.

"'That same phantom,' said the grandmother, 'appeared one time to Juan. It would come out of that cluster of white oaks and would disappear right at the corner of that field. Another time we were coming back from a wedding, and it must have been about one in the morning when it crossed the road in front of us, and we followed it until it disappeared behind a pile of posts that was there.'

"'Yes, *comadrita* [godmother],' commented another woman who had several beautiful daughters, 'that is why I lock up my daughters very early and barricade the door,' while the rest of the women continued making their own comments.

"But let us leave the women lamenting the incident and see what happened with the phantom. The poor boy was just beginning to talk after recovering from shock, which had left him mute. There united were all of the people from the ranch armed with rifles, pistols, machetes, and *macanas*.[2] An elderly man who was extremely religious had a small statue of *el santo niño* [the holy child, Jesus] and placed it at the head of the trail where the phantom had been seen.

"Suddenly and very excitedly someone in the back cried,

'Here comes the phantom!' 'Where?' cried the old man who was carrying the statue, jumping so high he appeared to have been thrown from a spring and so scared he dropped the santo niño. Now the phantom was getting closer and making such weird movements that everyone present was very afraid. The phantom continued on the trail until it came out into a small open area. Immediately an order was given to all of the families to return to their homes and barricade their doors, especially those with young girls, because the phantom was already in the middle of the ranch. Meanwhile, prayers and laments were heard throughout the homes, and many people were pounding their chest asking for forgiveness. Others were making promises to the *Virgen del Chorrito*.[3] In fact, there was such a commotion that it seemed that they had been attacked by Indians.

"But amid all that fear and wailing, suddenly there appeared two men who were not alarmed. They were determined to close in on the phantom, wanting to know the meaning of all this and noting that the stock had not been frightened. They inferred from this that the vision might be one of the local animals. Actually, it was a black cow from the ranch nicknamed 'the Blackbird' wrapped in a very white sheet. She had a problem freeing herself from the cloth! What we never did find out was how or when poor 'Blackbird' got tangled up in that rag and ended up looking like a phantom."

Mr. and Mrs. Stafford liked this true story very much and laughed a lot. We retired very pleased and met again the following day, when Mrs. Stafford's own story would begin.

Notes

1. A member of the cactus family, tasajillo has various names, including pencil cactus, rat-tail cactus, jumping cactus, and Christmas cactus.

2. A macana is a wooden club used as a weapon by the ancient Indians of Mexico and Peru.

3. The Virgen del Chorrito is a very popular virgin in Mexican Catholicism.

Chapter 7

Where We Will Hear the True Story of That Mysterious Petite Woman

T HE FOLLOWING EVENING at 7, Mrs. Stafford started to share with us her story in the following manner. "My parents were very poor, and, to make matters worse, my loving mother passed away when Elena, my older sister, was 7 years old and I was only 5. My father was very young when mother passed away, for he was barely 31 years of age. Mr. Nollen, my father's name, endured a great deal taking care of us and was deprived of many things until he had a beautiful idea: to install my sister and me in a convent in Victoria, Texas, the town where we were born. We were admitted, and my poor father now had more time to attend to his business as a Singer sewing machine salesman. He visited us often, and he would bring us clothing and presents, which would make us very happy. The mother superior liked us very much and nicknamed us the 'little orphan girls.'

"We started school at the convent. My sister was rapidly advancing in her studies, and so was I, swiftly passing from grade to grade. When she was in the tenth grade, I was right behind her in the eighth grade. When Elena was fifteen years old, she was accepted at the University of St. Louis, Missouri; I was also preparing to follow in her footsteps.

"I learned Spanish there. Our instructor was a nun who was born and raised in México, so she spoke Spanish perfectly. She would also teach us about the politics and governmental problems of México. That is why I was up to date on what was happening in our sister nation. There I made many little Mexican friends because, when I was fourteen or fifteen years old, I became their instructor. Among them was a precious little child about ten years of age who liked me very much. She was one of the most advanced among them, and frequently Mother Consuelo would select her to assist me. She could speak English well by that time. Her name was Brígida Cano, whose name I could never forget because my father told us a story of his motherland: Ireland.[1] His father was Irish and used to say the Irish have a belief in a saint to whom all of them pray for good luck in whatever endeavor or trips they made. They would all commend themselves to Saint Brígida. Every time I would see Brígida, it reminded me of my own ancestors, and that memory probably made me like her immensely—she was also an orphan and had only her mother. Anyway, whatever the reason, that creature was like an angel to me."

Then I interrupted her and told her I knew a child residing at Misión del Refugio who was also named Brígida, but I could not remember her last name. "I believe," said Mrs. Stafford, "she must be the same child because I remember she told me she was brought from that place to this convent, where the school was."

"Continuing my story, my sister went on to the University of St. Louis, and a year later I also entered the same university. There I studied medicine, and when I became a nurse, we both left at the same time, but she established herself in Galveston, and I went to San Antonio to be in charge of the Santa Rosa Hospital. I had been at the hospital for about eight months when a terrible railroad accident happened between Dallas and Houston, causing many fatalities and injuries, where among them was my husband-to-be, who is now present. He was so badly injured that doctors feared for his life because he had lost his voice and was unconscious. He had internal injuries, and the consensus was that he was a dead man. There was a general call for nurses from the surrounding cities and towns, and the Santa Rosa Hospital sent me as their representative, giving me full authority to use all my knowledge and act according to my experience. As soon as I arrived, they took me directly to see this patient, who was barely breathing. I carefully examined him, and then one of the many doctors who had come to help the injured from this terrible catastrophe asked my opinion on this patient's condition. I answered that this was a critical but not a fatal case."

"'Is it possible?' he asked, very much alarmed, as he started to leave, and he said he would come later to see him, and we continued helping the rest of the patients.

"Dr. Paschal, who came representing the Santa Rosa Hospital, was also my superior authority and had said to me: 'Attend to that patient. Do not leave him alone until I return.' I started by giving him an elixir to help him breath easier. Then I noticed he was putting his hand on his waist. I guessed he was possibly hurting there, and I began giving him tender massages with warm pads. One of the other nurses helped me to turn him on his side to begin the healing. I was very busy doing this job when I was called to the consulting office. There were six doctors around a table, and Dr. Paschal was at the head. As soon as he saw me he said: 'Anita, Dr. Boyd just told us that, in your examination of Mr. Stafford, you felt that he is not near death as is shown by his condition.' 'Yes, sir,' I answered, 'and now that I have been by his side for a few minutes, I feel more convinced he is not in agony.' 'Excellent,' said Dr. Paschal. 'Continue by his side. We will be there within five minutes to reexamine him.'

"I then returned to my patient and continued my massages; he surprised me by moaning. For me, this was a sign that there was life in him, and that made me very happy, for I had not made a mistake in my experiments on him. Then the doctors returned and very carefully reexamined him and found some improvement. It had been only about an hour since they had first examined him. About ten minutes later Dr. Paschal said to me: 'Anita (that is how he addressed me at the Santa Rosa Hospital), take this patient under your care and continually attend to him. Be at his side day and night. Of course, there will be someone to relieve you but only for you to rest and sleep.' 'Yes, sir, I will be glad to do what you order me,' I answered. 'I wish we could take him to our hospital,' said Dr. Boyd, who was the eldest of the doctors, and he proceeded to say, 'there we would have access to everything we need—you would have everything at your beck and call that was necessary.'

"'Anyway, I will try to keep in contact with you,' I told Dr. Boyd. 'That is fine, Anita. Do you have a special request from San Antonio you would like me to carry out?' Dr. Boyd asked before he left. 'No, sir, only for you to have a good trip.' 'Thank you,' the doctor answered and then added, 'I will try to come as frequently as I can unless I am urgently needed, but in that case you will be the one to call me.' 'I will try not to bother you, but I do not think it will be necessary. Anyway, I will notify you if there is any danger. I have a lot of faith that this patient will be saved. But, oh, my God! I seem to have missed something.' 'What is it? What are you missing, Anita?' the doctor asked me. 'Sir, I need a place to pray and ask God for the health and life of our patients. This would be invaluable for me because I have faith in God that our patient will soon get well.'"

As she was saying this, Mr. Stafford interrupted her and said, "My beloved, you have never told me this. It is so beautiful!" "I did not tell you," she said, "because I remember, when we promised to love each other forever, the first understanding we had when we were united in matrimony was that we mutually agreed we would respect each other's religious beliefs." "That is true," said Mr. Stafford, "but what you are saying with respect to your patients is sublime, and it is much bigger than what I imagined of your nobleness. But please continue with your story."

"Well, as I was saying," proceeded Mrs. Stafford, "I told the doctor I needed a place to pray, and immediately he communicated with the president of the center, and both came to consult with me about what I desired. I then told the superior of the needs we religious people had with regard to our prayers to God, even if the whole world identified us as fanatics, but I did not care how they might censure us because it was not justified. Besides, if ever sick people need spiritual help, it is when they are gravely ill, but many times it is a salvation to have a pious person ask His Divine Majesty for the patient's broken body to be returned to a healthy condition. 'Dear,' the mother superior answered, very moved, 'in this case I will provide you with whatever you request. Ask for it, and you shall have it.' 'All I need,' I answered the mother superior, 'is just a small place where I will not be disturbed during my prayers.' 'That's fine,' answered the mother superior, 'I will instruct them to prepare an adequate place to comply with your wishes.' 'Thank you, ma'am,' I said to the superior, 'and you, doctor, would you be so kind as to tell the superior of the Santa Rosa convent to mail me the needed items for me to properly arrange my praying center when you get back?' 'Very well,' said the doctor as he departed.

"The following day at 10 in the morning, I received a package that contained what I had requested. Then I was shown the place where I was to pray. I thought it was ideal, and it was close to my patient's room. Then I arranged it temporarily and made my first solemn prayers at 2 that same day. I remained in my prayer room for one hour and spent the rest of the afternoon sitting and very happy. Later I put clean clothes on my patient after I scrubbed his body with a sponge. The doctor came at 5:30, examined him very carefully, and said: 'Anita, what do you think of our patient?' 'I believe he is getting better,' I answered. 'But he does not talk or moan, and I believe it is time for him to react.' 'Yes, doctor,' I said, 'but it is also time for him to turn to the worst.' A little while later and after a close observation, the doctor said, 'it looks like the inflamed parts around his waist are less swollen now. He has removed his hand from his waist. It would be nice if we could x-ray him, but tonight I will administer a few drops of an elixir. At first, it will be every hour, then every two hours, and his heartbeat will indicate the progress or regress of his cure, and tomorrow morning at 9:30 we will x-ray him. I think that will be easier.' 'That is good,' I said, and then I went to the telephone to notify Dr. Paschal, who was at the Santa Rosa Hospital, what we had decided to do with our patient. He said it was okay and wanted to be present but that he would not arrive until 10, so he asked that we wait for him. After this, I talked to my patient's personal doctor and told him not to come back until 5. I began giving our patient his first medication and continued doing this until the third dose, then the fourth one at midnight.

"Around 1 in the morning, I was surprised when I heard him moan, and this made me happy because it was a good sign. I was there at his bedside, and immediately I asked him how he felt. He did not answer, and then I checked his pulse and noted it was getting weaker. I continued administering the other dose, and I noticed he was swallowing it much easier. The doctor came in at 5 and said, 'How is it going?' 'Well,' I answered, and we went directly to the writing desk, where we kept all of his records. I knew all of the reports were favorable, and I felt very elated when the doctor was reading them. He instantly exclaimed, 'Good! These reports indicate the patient has improved since he took those drops.' 'It appears he is beginning to feel,' I told the doctor. 'He has moaned quite loudly several times.' 'That is necessary,' he said. 'Let us prepare everything before Dr. Paschal arrives. We must have everything ready.'

"Before he departed, the doctor left instructions for all of the medications to be given to our patient. I followed all of the instructions to the letter. I continued applying tender massages, and then I noted he was in severe pain around his neck. I thought that might be the reason he could not talk and started applying warm linen to the back of his neck and face and gave him his medicine as instructed. At 7:45 the doctor came, looked at the patient, and asked me how he was doing, and I told him that everything indicated that he was slowly improving. Then the doctor said, 'But I cannot explain why he cannot speak, even if it is softly.' At that moment I showed him the back of the patient's neck and told him the patient appeared to feel something every time I rubbed that area. The doctor answered that this might be the reason why the patient could not speak but that we would soon know.

"A stretcher was prepared to transport our patient to where an X-ray machine was available. When the doctor from San Antonio arrived, we made some X-ray photos, which showed a black mark over his spine and very pronounced marks around his neck and waist area. They could not find any broken bones right away. When the patient began to speak, he said his legs were very painful, which was the reason he had to remain in the hospital for seven months before he was released. I remained at his side this whole time, and I will continue to be at his side for the rest of my life because we are united forever. Seeing him in good health and enjoying a sweet happy life makes me happy. The doctors kept on prescribing medication that my patient needed, and two weeks after the X rays were taken, he began to move his eyes and wanted to speak but could not. Then I wrote something on paper, and he asked me for a pencil and paper and intended to write but was not able to. He was very weak, so I did not allow him to try. About six weeks later, he began to talk and would show me where he was in pain. At last, after a long and painful convalescence, he was in almost perfect condition.

"Then, one day after about twenty-six weeks of being in the hospital, he told me, after a morning shower and sitting comfortably on a leather-covered elbow chair made especially for him, 'Oh God, I feel so good that I will dare to ask you a question. If I like your answer, you will make me the happiest mortal on earth.' However, before I go on, I must say that Dr. Paschal had told me beforehand that the patient under my care was a very rich man, a very powerful magnate in the railroad business, and without any relatives. And in case of his death, all of his wealth would go to the state or to some charitable institution because he was not religious. After sharing this information, let us get back to my story.

"When he mentioned he wanted to ask me a question, I answered, 'What is it you wanted to ask me? Well, feel free to ask. Since you are an honorable man, it will not inconvenience me to answer any question you wish to ask.' 'Are you sure, Anita?' he said, very pleased. 'Yes, sir, with all my heart,' I answered. 'Thank you, my dear. Now, this is my question. Would you like to be my wife if I would ask for your hand in marriage?' 'Oh, my God! Is this a dream or is it real? Sir, I thank you a thousand times for honoring me and considering me worthy of your wish. I will say it again. I offer my sincere thanks for honoring me with such a request, and I will answer you, but please listen to me for a few moments. As you already know, I have my father, who worries about me, and my sister, who is a doctor practicing her profession in a Galveston hospital and whose name is Elena Nollen and whom you already know, as she has frequently come to visit me. Now then, I will contact my father and my sister concerning your wish. If they both agree, I will give you my hand in marriage with all my heart because I know that your wish to marry me is sincere and well intentioned.'

"When I finished talking, he held my hand and placed it over his heart firmly but sweetly. 'Thank you, baby, but in the meantime, we will be just good friends until our love dreams become a reality, right?' And as he was saying this, he tried to get up, and I offered my arm as usual and helped him back to his bed. Then he asked for his newspaper and thanked me for it. 'I am now going to my desk,' I said, 'but if you need me, call right away.' 'You go about your business, Anita. I feel very good.'

"As soon as I went back to my desk, I began writing my father and my sister to tell them about the marriage proposal Mr. Stafford had made. On the third day, instead of receiving an answer, I happily received a visit from Elena and, a little later, one from my father. Elena was coming from Galveston, and my father from Victoria, Texas. Both, without communicating with each other, decided to visit me to talk about this issue in person.

"That evening we all met at a very special place to talk about such a delicate subject. Right away my father told me he would gladly agree for me to marry as soon as possible. After all, Mr. Stafford would make a desirable partner, was immensely rich, and had no family, and as his wife, I would be his only heir. In addition, my father said he knew Mr. Stafford was not a religious man but that would not keep him from being an honorable man. Besides, he was a very powerful and well-known man throughout the United States. Furthermore, his last brother had been a congressman. My sister, Elena, was very pleased with my good luck, telling me that God would always reward good people. She believed God had intervened in this miracle. We then went to visit Mr. Stafford to give him my answer. I took the initiative by saying to him, 'Mr. Stafford, this small and humble group, which is composed of my father, my sister, and myself, has come to give you the answer to your request that I marry you. I have discussed the matter with them, and they are in agreement with me that we accept with honor your request and your everlasting love for me. So, as soon as possible, we can set a wedding date, which will forever be the happiest day of my life.' Then my father spoke in the following manner: 'I am very happy my daughter sincerely agrees to become your wife, and I completely approve of all of her words. I do not hesitate in thanking you very sincerely for the honor you have bestowed on her by becoming her husband. It is a title that will fill her with joy and happiness, as she knows you will always love her because you are frank and noble, as proven by the fact that you have chosen as a life companion such a humble woman as my daughter. With all that now said, I will offer my wholehearted acceptance so that my daughter may become your wife.'

"When my father finished talking, he sat down. Then Mr. Stafford asked my sister, 'Dr. Nollen, have you anything to say?' 'Yes, sir, plenty!' responded Elena, 'but having had the honor of hearing Mr. Nollen, what he just now said is exactly what I would have said. Therefore, I will make mine each word that he said. And I will also offer my total agreement, as we have seen those dreams in your hearts crowned by sweet reality.' Then Elena, after speaking her thoughts, also sat down. Then Mr. Stafford stood up and expressed himself like this: 'Respectable young ladies, respectable Mr. Nollen, at this moment I am the happiest man on earth, the most fortunate of all mortals. I have made my determination from the deepest place in my soul to marry Miss Anita Nollen because I have the pleasure of knowing that she is a good, noble woman who has patiently, exquisitely, and delicately attended to my needs during the time I have been combating my grave illness. She has treated me with kindness and so much care that the best way to repay her is to give her my heart, as I am doing at this time, and thankfully you two have consented to let us marry and become man and wife. We shall become companions for life. For this, Anita, I am very grateful to you with all my heart.'"

(At this moment Mrs. Stafford paused to tell us that she guarded her husband's speech as a sacred relic ever fresh in her mind. Her husband then asked her, "Anita, is it possible I made such a speech?" "Certainly, dear," said Mrs. Stafford. Meanwhile her face turned as red as a rose as she proceeded to share her story.)

"After we had talked, my father asked when the wedding was to take place. My husband answered that it would be within two weeks because the doctors had told him that he would be completely well by that time. [He then added,] 'Of course, my doctors also told me to stay away from my former railroad business, and they have suggested that I turn to the land, choose a place of my liking, and raise some type of domestic animal. They also forbade me from living in the city.'

"Two weeks after these events took place, we met again, my sister having gone to Galveston to bring a priest to unite us in matrimony. Elena was our maid of honor, and Dr. Paschal was the best man. After the priest united us forever, my father offered his blessing, followed by warm congratulations from all of our friends at the hospital, where the wedding ceremony was held. A carriage was already waiting for us outside, took us for a ride around the city, and brought us back to the hotel for supper. After this, a special room was prepared for us at the lower part of the hotel, and we left for the theater. Our happy wedding took place on February 28, 1889.

"On the day of our wedding, we promised my father we would visit him, and we planned to keep our commitment as promised. The following day we went to the station to wait for the train that went to San Antonio, as we wanted to visit the Santa Rosa Hospital. When we arrived at the Santa Rosa, we received a warm reception from all of the nuns and from many of my husband's friends. We received many invitations to go out to dinner, but we accepted the one from the nuns of the hospital because it was important for me, and the dinner was abundant and exquisite. After supper, the religious community gave us their blessings. After all, it was a solemn occasion.

"They showered us with congratulations, and that made us very happy and joyful. The private room they offered us was like a paradise, for we had everything that we needed there. I spent the following day with the religious community, and my husband went out to take care of some business affairs at the banks and with the railroad companies. The following day, we boarded the train to Galveston, where Miss Elena Nollen, doctor of medicine, was waiting for us.[2] She had prepared an excellent supper for us in a beautiful apartment. There she introduced us to many of her friends, who welcomed us and warmly congratulated us. Everyone was challenging each other for the honor of being our hosts, but Dr. Nollen convinced them that this time it was her honor to be our host. After supper we went for a stroll at the dock because at that time it was a beautiful place to visit. From there we went to the opera, then returned to our apartment at 11:30, and my sister went to hers but not until we promised to meet at the Port Bolívar Restaurant for breakfast.

"That is what we did the following morning, and after breakfast my husband left to attend to important business with financiers and representatives from the railroad company. At noon we got together again, then went to the beach, where my godmother was giving a special lunch that consisted of fish, oysters, different vegetables, and a variety of fruits in season. There they also served us the traditional coastal coffee, identified as *caracolillo*, exported from Tuxpán, Veracruz, México. My husband loved that coffee, and my sister was aware of his preference, so she made it a point to see it was specially prepared for the occasion. This lunch was a splendid banquet, and my husband enjoyed it so much that, in a burst of enthusiasm, he exclaimed, 'No wonder it has been said that the appetite grows when you are near the sea! What do you say to that, doctor?' 'I say that when you are always near the sea, the stomach becomes weaker.' 'Then it is true what has been said about sailors, that they are well known for being gluttons,' I said as I was taking part in the conversation. Elena said, 'What they are—is handsome. When I visited a ship on its way to India, I met a navy captain, and in my judgment there is no doubt about what I am saying. It has been already three weeks since I met this young captain, who was on his way to distant lands, and I am concerned for his well-being. As he left, he told me they needed a doctor aboard the ship, and he wished I would be that doctor, as he lightly squeezed my hand, bringing it up to touch his heart as he was saying a sweet good-bye.' 'Please forgive me, doctor, but I see you are in love.' 'Yes, Anita, and instead of saying what was said a moment ago—that they are heavy eaters— you should have said they fall in love easily.' We all laughed with good humor, especially when we realized that those remarks might be the preliminaries for a possible wedding.

"After we finished lunch, we went to our respective lodgings, and Elena promised to meet us again at 6, after she had seen some of her homebound patients. My husband went to finish his personal affairs because we had to travel south the following morning to visit my father as we had promised.

"At 6:30 the three of us met again and went for dinner at the Port Bolívar Restaurant and visited the O'Corner [O'Connor] family, who had known us since the time when mother was still living.³ They had assisted us greatly when she was very sick and then at her funeral. My grateful sister, Elena, had promised to visit them. We invited my husband to accompany us and described to him the people we would be going to visit. He happily went with us.

"Mrs. O'Connor, who was a very well-to-do and very religious person, welcomed us with great joy and many attentions. Mrs. O'Connor kindly told my husband that 'when people are good, God helps them. The parents of Anita, your dignified wife, were perhaps the poorest family in the neighborhood where they lived, but they were known for their impeccable honesty, a virtue appreciated by all. Her mother was a saintly woman who was worthy of consideration and respect from all who knew her, and God had to reward her actions.'

"Thereafter we continued talking about many other subjects, and among them was how the doctors had recommended that my husband not live in a city or town and that he abandon all ties with the railroad business and dedicate himself to raising farm or ranch stock of any kind. He needed to live out in the open country so that his tired mind would be stimulated. 'And now,' my husband told Mrs. O'Connor, 'we are going to Victoria to see if we can find a good place to live.' Then Mrs. O'Connor told my husband about the agents she had in Victoria, who could show him some property she owned in that county, since that is where she was born. 'If you like one of those properties,' said Mrs. O'Connor, 'you can immediately take possession of it. I also have much land in other counties so you can choose the place you like.'

"After all that was said, we decided to leave Mrs. O'Connor at about 10 and then went back to our place to retire for the evening. The train we were supposed to board the following morning to Victoria would be by very early, before 6:30, so we had to be ready by then. As planned, we went to the railroad station in the company of Elena and had breakfast there at the station restaurant. The train arrived on time. We immediately boarded but not until we exchanged a tender good-bye with my sister, Elena, promising to see each other soon because she was also planning to visit my father.

"We arrived at Victoria at noontime, and Mr. Nollen was already there, waiting for us with many of his friends and a large number of my husband's friends. My father had already prepared a huge lunch at the home of a friend of ours. After we had dinner, we received a great number of friends who came to congratulate us and express their joy in knowing that such a dignified family was coming to be part of their community. We in turn thanked them for this undeserved praise, ending their visit at 3, at which time we went to visit the convent.

"The religious community was already waiting for us since my father had previously made them aware of our visit. They had prepared luxurious lodgings for us where we could stay as long as we wished to be in the city. The nuns received us with much kindness and announced they had a big surprise for me since I had been one of their favorite students and had studied at this convent to enter the University of St. Louis, where I had received a degree in nursing. They had planned a blessing ceremony and led us to a special location where the blessing was to take place. However, we felt very contrite.

"After this solemn religious ceremony, my father and my husband left, concerned about the arrangements needed to find a place where my husband and I could settle. They went to look for the salesmen, who showed them some tracts of land near the city. But one of Mrs. O'Connor's agents told my husband that this lady had a property encompassing 210 acres in Columbus [Colorado] County in a place known as 'Altair.' This land was a beautiful place and superior to all that they had already seen. Then my husband told the agent that he wished to see that place, and they agreed to take the train the following morning that was to go to Cuero at 6. There they would connect to another road to go to the aforementioned place. This was done, but once out of Cuero, the agent told them they had to return to Cuero that afternoon and would not have time to return to their homes. After having seen and examined the land, my husband told the agent to take them back and that he would see that they got back to Victoria that same evening. As it actually turned out, after they saw and examined the land, they returned to Cuero, where my husband hired a special coach that brought them home that evening as promised.

"As soon as my husband saw the land, he liked it very much and told me he thought there was not anything like it in the surrounding area. He also wanted to know if I liked it since he had to resolve the issue the following day. Naturally I told him that if he liked it, I would like it also. After all, we were going to buy one of Mrs. O'Connor's properties.

"The following day, the buy-sell contract for the land was processed, and then my father promised to build us the very home where we are at this very moment. From there we went to Dallas, where we had a lot of work to do. From then on, I became my husband's secretary, traveling to Forth Worth before returning to San Antonio. After six weeks, we came back to take possession of our new home, which was already finished. Our furniture was bought in Houston and shipped in an enclosed railroad car to our new home.[4]

"Some of the very first things we did for our new farm were to buy two hundred Rhode Island Red pullets. Those were the ones you first saw when you arrived at my home and that you mentioned you liked so much. Do you remember?"

"Yes, ma'am," I answered.

"Well," she continued, "I believe I have finished my story. I hope you have enjoyed it, and may it be of some help for your future." "I assure you, ma'am, that your story has been most interesting and very beautiful." Then I thanked her and Mr. Stafford.

The next day we continued our fence-building project until it was completed. As soon as we finished the fence, I went to Yoakum, where all of our tools and camping equipment were well stored in one of the farm's storage buildings. They were to be left there until I returned for them. Then Mr. Stafford took us over to Eagle Lake to board our train. Since our jobs in Yoakum had been completed, the workers all went every which way as they pleased. I had many good friendships among the Mexican element in Yoakum, so I decided to remain there for a good while.[5]

End of the First Volume

Notes

1. In later years, Brígida Cano became the wife of Luis Gómez.
2. Research for this translation failed to reveal a Dr. Elena Nollen in Galveston. It did, however, locate an Ellen Mullen, midwife, in that city for this particular period. See *Galveston City Directory, 1890–1891* (Galveston: Morrison and Fourmy), 484.
3. Although the name O'Corner appears in the original Spanish text, we have chosen to change it to O'Connor, the name of prominent landowners in the Victoria area during the period and to whom the author most likely referred.
4. Although a prominent family named Stafford was responsible for founding the community of Altair in Colorado County during the 1880s, a careful examination of the Stafford family history and genealogy in that region by Bill Stein, local historian and director of the Nesbitt Memorial Library in Columbus, Texas, county seat of Colorado County, found no similarities between Luis Gómez's rendition and the origins of the known Stafford family members. Perhaps Gómez's memory may not have served him well about the actual names of the couple who had befriended him some forty-five years before he published his memoirs. Or perhaps the Stafford couple of whom Gómez spoke was a different family from the founder of the settlement. Regardless of the particulars, Luis Gómez, a man of great veracity, no doubt correctly recalled the general aspects of this incident when, as a young stranger sojourning in Colorado County, he received assistance from a husband and wife of much stature and kindness. See Bill Stein to Tom Kreneck, Feb. 7, 2002, Donor Files on Luis G. Gómez, *Mis Memorias,* Special Collections and Archives, Mary and Jeff Bell Library, Texas A&M University–Corpus Christi. Bill Stein, telephone conversation with Thomas H. Kreneck, Apr. 25, 2005.
5. Note by Javier Villarreal: While I adhered to the spirit of Guadalupe Valdez's translation of his grandfather's original text, in my editing I have also conformed to Luis G. Gómez's original Spanish narrative as I understood it, hoping to relay the primary author's intent: to entertain. As a nonscholarly document, Gómez's volume exhibits inconsistencies mainly in sentence structure and punctuation, presenting numerous ambiguities for the reader. I have made sure, however, that three important features are present in this English version. First, I have ensured that more Spanish words are left in the English text because they enrich the final product. Second, I insisted that the translation follow the structure presented in Gómez's original manuscript as much as possible. And third, any new punctuation included in this English translation comes only where the message might otherwise be compromised, thus allowing the reader to experience the flavor of the original with all its ups and downs. To ease the reading experience, certain paragraphs simply had to be shortened

and, as noted before, some names have been changed to reflect their original spelling in English. For those readers who want to experience the fullness of Luis Gómez's language, I join with Kreneck and Valdez in inviting them to inspect the original Spanish version in the Special Collections and Archives of Texas A&M–Corpus Christi. On a personal note, I was struck by the manner in which this monograph depicts the real-life experiences of a person in Central Texas who was trying to survive in the latter part of the nineteenth century. It thus presents an invaluable source of historical and sociological information from a perspective seldom seen: the working-class *mexicano*.

Index

INDEX

CPSIA information can be obtained at www.ICGtesting.com
Printed in the USA
LVOW07s2006200115

423629LV00001B/2/P